Three Women Walk Into a Bar . . .

Three Women Walk Into a Bar . . .

A Community Responds to a Bias Attack

An Email Chronicle

Karin Barnaby

ISBN 978-0-615-37210-5

The test of courage comes when we are in the minority.
The test of tolerance comes when we are in the majority.

-- Ralph W. Sockman, *Wickipedia*

CONTENTS

ACKNOWLEDGEMENTS

Sooner or later, willingly or unwillingly, we get caught up in an event whose significance transcends our personal day-to-day lives. Despite our good intentions, we often lack the energy and resolve to speak up and follow through with an effective response. Such engagement becomes almost effortless as soon as other likeminded individuals join us in a common purpose.

I am most grateful to my husband, Doug, my staunchest support and ally, for his encouragement and participation in the Sea Cliff Tolerance Rally.

"Adam's" immediate and utterly likeminded engagement transformed a solitary call for action into a successful community activism. Without his clarity, courage and energy we could not have succeeded.

"Angela" provided everything a wise guardian angel possibly could: encouragement, guidance, participation and, most of all, an unflagging validation of purpose.

"The Smiths'" spontaneous essay on collective responsibility provided the essential philosophical justification, at just the right moment, for this as well as every worthwhile community activism.

FOREWORD

Society's dissonances and harmonies are repeated at every interpersonal level, much like the patterns on Russian nesting dolls are repeated on the largest through to the tiniest one. These email communications, compiled by Karin Barnaby, illustrate how society is more than the sum of its social relationships and, instead, appears to be responsive, as in the butterfly effect, where small changes exert a large influence on the system as a whole. The iconic photograph, circa 1989, of a single person facing down a row of tanks on Tiananmen Square is an obvious example. Someone disclosing their sexual orientation (coming out) may not be as obvious. In both of these examples, however, the genie has left the bottle and those who bear witness are potentially changed forever.

Readers of this volume are encouraged to explore their own reactions to a broad spectrum of responses to a bias incident in a small community. Some, like the subjects of this chronicle, will be inspired, others incensed. Some will maintain their silence and others will give up the privilege their silence affords, to explore the meaning of tolerance and courage.

The actor and playwright Harvey Fierstein, in a 2007 New York Times Op-ed entitled "Our Prejudices, Ourselves," stated: "I urge you to look around, or better yet, listen around and become aware of the prejudice in everyday life. [. . .] Prejudice tolerated is intolerance encouraged. Rise up in righteousness when you witness the words and deeds of hate, but only if you are willing to rise up against them all, including your own."

Diane Bruessow

PREFACE

Two groups of young people clashed at a bar in Sea Cliff, my hometown, on Labor Day weekend, 2007. Newspapers, television reports and Internet postings worldwide headlined the incident as a "bias-motivated assault," an "anti-gay attack," a "hate crime." The incident involved television celebrity, Josie Smith-Malave, who had competed on the reality show, "Top Chef," and who is openly gay.

For as long as I've known Sea Cliff—and I've known it for more than 40 years—it has been a live-and-let-live community, a haven for non-conformists, a nurturer of artists. The town I know and love embraces diversity, creativity and eccentricity. The shocking headlines, however, suggested another, less tolerant aspect.

There have been times when I remained silent in the face of some wrong or injustice because I was not directly affected or because I felt embarrassed, impotent or not certain enough—it was the wrong time or place; no one cared; it wouldn't make a difference anyway. Excuses are always plentiful.

This time, however, the hateful words and actions of a handful of individuals directly reflected on me, on my friends, neighbors and community. I wanted to repudiate this prejudicial act and reaffirm Sea Cliff's tradition of tolerance. So I voiced my outrage in the most immediate and direct way I know, via email, to friends, acquaintances and, eventually, to a much larger community of like-minded—and not so like-minded—individuals and groups that extended far beyond our village. Our community's response—including its evolution from emotional reaction as a "protest," to its eventual realization as a "tolerance rally"—was organized almost entirely via emails.

In this email chronicle, about 50 individuals, most of them strangers to each other, react to news of the attack and deliberate on an appropriate response. Reactions run the gamut from rationalization to outrage; from blame-the-victim judgments about the women's behavior to dismay on the part of the lesbian and gay community; from ridicule and graphic hate mail to astonishingly clear-eyed essays about individual behavior and collective responsibility.

I don't know to what degree emails, as non-fiction-project, have been explored or experimented with by others. Here, their dynamics and energy approximate those of a musical composition, of a complex fugue, in which various motifs sound and fade against the point and counterpoint of the main themes. Unrelated dissonances threaten the desired harmony with greater or lesser intensity, only to be drowned out again by the unexpected beauty and brilliance of familiar or fresh new voices and motifs, all culminating in a harmonious and stirring resolution.

I don't know what happened to the young people involved, who were not charged. Nor do I know the details of the legal proceedings against those who were arrested, beyond the fact that they were all released eventually. I left a message with the victim on her website, but did not get a response.

I've changed all the names but my husband's and mine. Some individuals explicitly requested that their actual names be used, as well. The emails appear in their original form—typos and all—but not always in chronological order, i.e., in the chaotic sequence in which they arrived and were sent. I have grouped them thematic-ally and annotated them to flow more smoothly and logically for the reader.

Finally, I've included every expression of support, no matter how brief, clichéd, random or repetitive, because it was so important to me.

Three Women Walk Into a Bar . . .

Three Women Walk Into a Bar . . .

A Community Responds to a Bias Attack

An Email Chronicle

The news

I first learn of a bias incident in Sea Cliff, two weeks after it happened, when a friend who was born and raised in Sea Cliff, now living out of state, copies me and others on an email to her son, who is gay. She attaches a copy of a news report of the assault.

Date: Wed, 12 Sep 2007, 12:34
Subject: Check out Ex-'Top Chef' contestant is attacked- USATODAY.com

1 From Zoe to her son Nick
CC: Karin plus 33 contacts

Dear Nick,

A friend found this online. It breaks my heart that it happened in Sea Cliff. Apparently three women (two lesbians and the straight sister of one of them) were visiting and went to the bar that I would have described as low-down but not unsafe. It used to be the "High Ceiling" and your grandfather was once astonished to see a topless dancer when he stopped in for a pack of cigarettes. Two of these visitors started dancing, got treated abusively, and all three were hustled out the door and attacked on the sidewalk by a mob from the bar. It's tragic that this could happen anywhere and I wonder if it's only considered newsworthy because one of the women has minor celeb status. I'm so sad that you and Ethan need to consider your safety just about everywhere you go.

Please be careful, my dear.

Love,

Mom

Attachment:

Ex-'Top Chef' contestant is attacked

SEA CLIFF, N.Y. (AP) A former contestant on Bravo's *Top Chef* was
beaten by attackers yelling anti-gay slurs, her lawyer said. Josie Smith-
Malave, who was featured on the second season of the reality show, was
among a small group of women who were asked to leave a Sea Cliff bar
over Labor Day weekend, lawyer Yetta Kurland said Tuesday. About 10
young people followed the women and began screaming anti-gay
epithets, spitting on them and then beating them, Kurland said. Smith-
Malave, who is in her early 30s, is openly gay, Kurland said. Nassau
County police said they were investigating, but declined to provide details
of the incident. Smith-Malave, a Miami native, is a former sous-chef for
Marlow and Sons restaurant in Brooklyn. She has played for the New
York Sharks of the Independent Women's Football League.

Date: Wed, 12 Sep 2007, 13:37
Subject: Re: Check out Ex-'Top Chef' contestant is attacked

2 To Zoe from Karin

How very sad. This is not the Sea Cliff I know and love. So sorry.
Karin

Date: Wed, 12 Sep 2007, 16:27
Subject: Terrorism in the Homeland

3 To Karin Barnaby from Zoe

Of course it's not the Sea Cliff you know and love. And who *are* these
punks, and who are their parents? I'd like to sit down and have a
long chat with all of them.

This is what I just got back from a woman with whom I grew up [in Sea
Cliff]: "It was especially nice to see your note to Nick on this
recent forward about the terrible episode in Sea Cliff. It's not the
first time this kind of activity has taken place in Sea Cliff: in the 1950's
my brother was mercilessly harassed and beaten up in bars. But this is
2007--and that's the shock of it."

I'm pretty down about this, and I know you can handle my venting. Why
the hell didn't the barkeep toss out the hate criminals instead of the
victims? Why didn't the cops treat it more seriously? Why did it take over
a week to hit the newspapers?

I'll follow the progress of this case online and eventually I'll quit taking it
personally. Hoping that you and your lambs are all fine.
Love,
Zoe

Let's do something

I discuss the assault with my husband, Doug, and suggest organizing a demonstration at the place where it happened. With his encouragement, I send an email, including the news article, to my Sea Cliff contacts. Moments later, hoping to get the word out to more people, I send a second appeal to additional contacts listed in the address line of an email I'd recently received from a local organization. This decision would come to haunt me.

Date: Wed, 12 Sep 2007, 18:56
Subject: Let's do something

4 To 98 contacts from Karin

I just heard about this today. In case you have not heard, I'd like to call your attention to it. This kind of behavior is not acceptable in Sea Cliff or anywhere else. I would like to suggest a village-wide protest at Partners on Saturday, Sept. 15 at 7 p.m.
Karin Barnaby
Attachment: News article

Date: Wed, 12 Sep 2007, 19:30
Subject: Terrorism in the Homeland

5 To Zoe from Karin

Those "punks" are the slimy underbelly of every "nice" community. I do have to say that what I've seen go into & emerge from Partners are mostly smoking, drinking types. Still, this calls for some kind of action. I've emailed everyone I know the following, along with the article. Let's see what happens.
xoxo Karin

Date: Thu, 13 Sep 2007, 10:44
Subject: Terrorism in the Homeland

6 To Karin from Zoe

Thanks, Karin. You can always be counted on to know what the right thing to do is and then not just thinking about it, but actually doing it. I'll be interested to hear what kind of a turnout there is on Sat. evening at Opposite Sex Partners.
Zoe

Reactions
Outrage, caution, questions and a petition

Date: Wed, 12 Sep 2007, 20:16
Subject: Let's do something

7 To Karin from Jacob
hi karin.

count on me for saturday, 9/15/07. i saw it on the news today. how awful. would like to know who was involved.

love,

Jacob

Date: Wed, 12 Sep 2007, 21:49
Subject: Let's do something

8 To Karin from Bella
Pathetic.

Bella

Date: Wed, 12 Sep 2007, 22:14
Subject: Let's do something

9 To Karin from Elaine
Karin,

Do you know any more about this? Why were the women asked to leave the bar in the first place? Was there already some violence going on within the bar? Are any of the people involved, on either side of this dreadful mess, residents of Sea Cliff? I need more information before I would feel comfortable taking any action.

Thank you--

Elaine

Date: Thursday, September 13, 2007 10:15
Subject: Let's do something

10 To Karin from Corinne
Does anyone know exactly what happened? Are we assuming the media version is the truth??

Corinne

Date: Thu, 13 Sep 2007, 10:19
Subject: Protest at Partners Sat., 9/15, 7 p.m.

11 To Karin from Lily
I had not heard at all! This is repulsive. You are totally right, and I applaud you for your initiative. We are leaving for Maine tomorrow, until Next Monday evening, unfortunately. Where is PARTNERS? Was the behaviour of gay-bashing IN the bar, or just near it? Were the thugs customers of the bar at that time or were they just passing by?

Lily

12 To Karin from Vickie

Hi!

[A friend] got yr e-mail and passed it on to me. Congratulations for taking action! In response, i'm sending you as attachments to this e-mail 2 documents: An Open Letter to Sea Cliff, and, a Petition, in the hope that you'll endorse what is proposed therein and also pass it along. I'm not sure of the best way to do this via e-mail. Can we speak sometime tomorrow morning and perhaps coordinate our efforts? I look forward to meeting you at the protest gathering on Saturday.

All best,

Vickie

Vickie's Letter and Petition:

OPEN LETTER

September 12, 2007

Dear Neighbors,

    I think you know why I'm upset. The story that broke on Internet newswires Wednesday morning and is now being reported by network media about an attack on visitors to Sea Cliff has me shocked and deeply concerned. That a visitor to our village should be thrown out of a bar for dancing with a same sex partner, and then subsequently beaten by a group of young bar patrons as well as others, is an outrage that needs to be addressed by our community and its leaders at the highest levels.

    To my mind, this occurrence is a throwback to the days when my family first moved here, in 1950. At that time many parts of Long Island were off-limits to Jews, African-Americans, Latinos and other minorities. For all I know it was just as inhospitable to gays, except that in 1950 most gays living outside urban centers were closeted. Such is not the case today. Still, even then Sea Cliff was a community that welcomed diversity and practiced tolerance, with many of its residents engaged in the arts of music, painting, theatre, dance and literature. Then as now, ordinary citizens and businesses and elected officials worked tirelessly for the good of the village. Today, I practice the same respect for the privacy of my neighbors' personal lifestyle choices as they do for mine—we live in harmony with each other—but now I feel compelled to speak out.

There has been a bar on that corner for as long as I can remember. It has always been essentially a "working-class" bar as opposed to the more upscale establishments for which Sea Cliff has since become famous, establishments that serve people from near and far who come here to sample the outstanding food and friendly ambiance of our village. We can be proud of these places as well as the other businesses in town that contribute to Sea Cliff's unique reputation. The bars of which Partners is one and Gallagher's (the more family-oriented of the two) is the other, have been equally important parts of the egalitarian fabric of village life for many years. They also serve our citizens and go far toward making events like Fourth of July celebrations and Mini-Mart a success. However, let me remind you that doing business in Sea Cliff is not a right. A strong message must be sent to those who ignore the basic codes of conduct we all cherish. If we fail to act now, then the next outrage will be a cross burned on someone's lawn or a swastika painted on the side of someone's house.

Of course, not all the facts of the incident have come out yet. When they do, I sincerely hope that we learn why the victims were the ones asked to leave the premises, which amounted to tacit permission for the perpetrators to pursue and attack them, When the facts come out, I sincerely hope that the failure of the bar management to address this incident for what it was, an ugly example of hate crime violence, will be explained and that any persons including those who may have encouraged it and/or looked the other way, will be punished to the full extent of the law. When Nassau police come forward to make public all the facts of their investigation, I sincerely hope that the failure of our Sixth Precinct officers to arrest anyone at the scene, or soon thereafter, will also be explained.

The victims will seek their remedy in the courts, as they should. Until then, however, I think we need to come to grips with this ourselves. I'm asking that you join me in signing the following petition to our mayor, and the Village Board of Trustees. Please pass it around to as many of your friends and neighbors as possible. Karin Barnaby has suggested that we convene at Partners bar on Saturday, September 15, at 7 p.m., to protest the above events. I will be there to collect the petitions. I look forward to meeting you.

Vickie

PETITION

To the Mayor and Board of Trustees of the Village of Sea Cliff.
We, the undersigned, ask that you call for a public meeting to be held in a venue
such as one of our district's grade school auditoriums. We ask that you invite all
elements of our community to participate: residents, schools, churches,
businesses, law enforcement, local media and government. We ask that you
frame your call to meet as an invitation to address the cultural and safety issues
we face as a result of the recent event at Partners, so we can determine what
practical steps to take in order to discourage such things from happening again.
We need to collectively look within, as only citizens in a free society can do.
And, for our future and that of our children, we need to demonstrate Sea Cliff's
fundamental opposition to bigotry of any kind. Zero tolerance for intolerance
is the only answer.

Signed:

Name   Address

Adam

*I'd met Adam, a young teacher, husband and father of three, a few times at
community gatherings and we don't know each other well. He jumps right in
with two resolute emails. His youth, like-minded engagement and energy
make me hopeful that we can organize a powerful community response.*

Date: **Wed, 12 Sep 2007, 22:04**
Subject: Protest at Partners Sat., 9/15, 7 p.m.

13 To Karin from Adam
Well done. I'll be there.
Peace and Pay it Forward,
Adam

Date: **Wed, 12 Sep 2007, 22:07**
Subject: Protest at Partners Sat., 9/15, 7 p.m.

14 To Karin from Adam
Maybe we should make some sort of signs like "Not in this village" or
"Homophobics Stay Out" or something like that.
Peace and Pay it Forward,
Adam

15 To Adam from Karin

How about "Intolerance will not be tolerated & ignorance will not be ignored?"
Karin

16 To Adam from Karin

Thanks, Adam. You are one of the first to say you'll be there. Might just be the two of us. Let's see what happens.
Karin

17 To Karin from Adam

That's fine with me. It would be worth it. Great slogans. What do you think about asking PrintStars in the Dunkin Donut Shopping Center to donate a banner?
Adam

18 To Adam from Karin

I'm so happy that you are aboard on this, Adam. I had not thought in terms of a banner. Not sure what it should say. I was thinking more along the lines of reading a short forceful statement. It would be good to post fliers a.s.a.p. to encourage everyone to come to the rally, as well. Also, I think 6 p.m. would be a better time.
I have to go out for about 2 hours. I will devote myself totally to fliers, statement, banner, when I get back. Maybe we should talk. My number:
Karin

A candid exchange

Adam has the following animated e-mail exchange with his friend, Ken, whose cautious reaction reflects the lack of firsthand information and/or eyewitnesses. Together, Adam and Ken articulate some of the implications of the assault for the community and, for the first time, raise the question of the mayor's and trustees' official response.

19 To Adam from Ken

So what happened really? I am getting a lot of rumors through the mill.
Any first-hand knowledge?

K

20 To Ken from Adam

I don't know of any first hand knowledge as I'm not sure how many
people were actually at the attack (possibly 14?). Here is a link to an
article about what happened:

Former Top Chef contestant says she was viciously attacked for being
gay http://advocate.com/news_detail_ektid48786.asp

It seems that regardless of what actually transpired, there seems to be
pretty good evidence of a bias crime and I think we should act. We
should say that as a community this type of behavior is not acceptable
and that everyone is welcome here. I'm hoping we can change the
location from outside Partners to maybe a walk to Memorial Park. I'm
going to speak with Karin about that this morning (or tomorrow
morning, as I'm going back to bed) I hope you are doing well.

---By the way, [Village trustee] does not think it would be appropriate to
post this type of meeting on the Website. What do you think?

Peace and Pay it Forward,

Adam

21 To Adam from Ken

Hey Adam-

Yeah, I agree it's not a good thing to have happen in our little village.
Some versions of the story that I heard had the women acting very
uppity and making fun of some of the locals, which progressed into open
heckling back and forth and eventually, to them playing the age card in
having those kids ejected from the bar (some of whom waited outside to
exact revenge, apparently.) Who knows. I don't know any of the players
involved. I think my parents were interviewed on Sea Cliff Ave by
Channel 7 while walking the baby.

But, because I can't get any first-hand info on what happened I'm staying
cautiously neutral. It took place at a pub, after all, and a drinking pub at

that. Things happen when alcohol gets involved.

I'm going to have to agree with [Village trustee] on keeping it off the site - at least until it's resolved by the authorities. The alt-Sea Cliff site I've been wanting to put together would be a great spot for this. But who knows when THAT project is going to see the light of day!

Cheers,

Ken

Date: Saturday, September 15, 2007 12:02 AM
Subject: Sea Cliff rally for tolerance at 6 p.m.

22 To Ken from Adam

I really have to disagree. I would think that even if the women were piss drunk, dancing naked and taunting the locals with witchcraft, that wouldn't give anyone the right to beat them up while yelling homophobic remarks. It seems to me that a "rally" that is being organized to say that the people would not like it if the alleged allegations of the bias incident were committed in Sea Cliff could appear on the website. It just seems that What's New is supposed to be an informational service provided to community groups and the people of the Village. Last year, I was allowed to post my Long Islanders for a Department of Peace Walk without a problem. I just think it becomes dicey if the government begins to choose what is and what is not "appropriate." Anyway, for now the "rally" has been postponed for at least a week so that it can be better organized.

I hope you, your wife and your baby are doing well. Sleep when you can!

Peace,

Adam

Date: Saturday, September 15, 2007 12:18 PM
Subject: Sea Cliff rally for tolerance at 6 p.m.

23 To Adam from Ken

NO, no, no...I agree. Bias crimes and slurs and such are always crude and debase all of us. I read some of what a witness heard and it's really quite awful. I'm with you on that, no question. And the one comment overheard, "I hope you die of AIDS"... well, that's just downright unenlightened. I just don't know what prompted the argument/fight. Things said in the heat of passion (plus booze) are always terrible. Remind me to tell you about a 40+ person brawl I once witnessed simply because one guy knocked the sports-team hat off another. It took place at a pub of course!

As for the village website - you know we're on the same page (when I wanted to have the discussion group online but was shot-down, among other things). But unless it's a Village sanctioned-event, I don't know if it can go up there - especially around a charged subject. It's easier for [Village trustee] to acquiesce around benign topics (LI Dept of Peace). Perhaps if you get Village approval (read: get the Mayor to sign off on it), it can get posted. Has [Village trustee] raised the question to the Board? If it's that important to you, you should press for a formal yea or nay.
Ken

P.S. Everyone's doing well here, Conor just passed 1 month (I can't believe it) but we're still getting used to the new routines...and lack of sleep.

A thoughtful challenge

John, a local business owner, questions the idea of a protest at the bar. I do not initially welcome his probing emails—which are grouped together below—but his objections soon become extremely valuable to me. John's persistent challenge causes me rethink what it is that I want to accomplish. This forces me to articulate a clear purpose to him and, ultimately, to myself and to the community.

Date: Thu, 13 Sep 2007, 11:12
Subject: Protest at Partners Sat., 9/15, 7 p.m.

24 To Karin from John
Hi Karin,
While I believe that there is no place for discrimination or prejudice in our community, I have merely heard allegations with no evidence. According to the proprietor of Partners and the Nassau County Police two groups of people were asked to leave the bar due to poor behavior. Apparently these individuals engaged in a fight on the street (which both groups of people claim was started by the other).
Before a lynch mob is formed, I think the facts should be established. I am sure glad that when a certain individual claimed anti-Semitism against our neighbors that nobody formed protests assuming the allegations were credible.
John

25 To John from Karin

Hi, John.

I agree, this is no time for a lynch mob. I'm not sure how you reached that conclusion. The incident has been written up as a "bias-motivated assault outside a Sea Cliff bar" in *Newsday, USA Today* & Yahoo news, among many others. The intent here is to counteract the negative press and to allow the majority of Sea Cliff residents to repudiate the intolerant and ignorant words and actions of a few individuals while at the same time reaffirming Sea Cliff's long tradition of tolerance and fairness toward individuals of all backgrounds and persuasions. The purpose of the rally is to make a simple public statement to that effect.

Hope to see you there. Please note that we will meet at 6 p.m. and not at 7 as originally stated.

Karin

News update

Taking John's challenge to heart, I change the subject line of all subsequent emails to read "Sea Cliff rally for tolerance," instead of "Protest at Partners." Also, in my next group email, which includes a news update about, I include a statement of purpose taken directly from the rationale I'd articulated for John.

26 To 98 contacts from Karin

Please note that we will meet at Partners on Saturday 9/15 at 6 p.m. and not at 7 as originally stated. The purpose of Saturday's rally is to allow the majority of Sea Cliff residents to repudiate the intolerant and ignorant words and actions of a few individuals.

I'm including a *Newsday* article about a "bias-motivated assault outside a Sea Cliff bar." This is the second anti-gay crime in Nassau this year. According to this article, one of the women was kicked in the head, another dragged on the ground, the attackers yelled anti-gay slurs and stole a video camera. Someone said the bar was becoming "too gay."

Let's make this a simple yet resounding public statement to let the world know Sea Cliff is not like that. At the same time, it is an opportunity to reaffirm Sea Cliff's long tradition of tolerance and fairness toward individuals of all backgrounds and persuasions.

Hope to see you there.

Karin

Second thoughts.

I'd automatically assumed the appropriate community response was to protest the alleged assault at the place where it occurred. John's defense of the bar and its owner make me realize that my actions might do harm. My initial emotional reaction is evolving into a more thoughtful, positive purpose. My rewording of the subject line to read "rally for tolerance" is not lost on John. I'm reconsidering the location and timing of the rally, as well.

Date: Thu, 13 Sep 2007, 16:09
Subject: Protest at Partners Sat., 9/15, 6 p.m.

27 To Karin from John

Karin,

You called for a "village-wide protest at Partners," not a rally. A protest is defined as a complaint, objection, gripe, dissent or opposition; and is generally a negative (or divisive) event. A rally is defined as a meeting, gathering, or assembly; and is usually a positive (or uniting) event.

The coverage of the anti-Semitism case in *Newsday, USA Today, The NY Times, ABC News, NBC News, CBS News* and many more was presented as a bias-motivated violation of someone's civil rights. I am extremely grateful that these accusations did not result in protests on Sea Cliff Avenue.

Furthermore, the proprietor of Partners has not been accused of any wrongdoing so why should she have to deal with protestors outside her establishment?

I am just as outraged as anybody that there is such intolerance in this day and age. But, let's be careful not to victimize any innocent bystanders while expressing our upset.

Thanks for considering my thoughts on this matter.

John

Date: Thu, 13 Sep 2007, 16:16
Subject: Protest at Partners Sat., 9/15, 6 p.m.

28 To John from Karin

Please forgive me, John. I am trying very hard to refine and clarify thoughts while trying to do the right thing.

Karin

29 To Karin from John

Karin,

I am with you. I understand where you are coming from (I have very close friends and family who are gay). Having a store next door to Partners gives me a birds-eye view of the pain these accusations have caused a broad range of people.

John

30 To John from Karin

John,

From what I know, whatever happened between two possibly drunk groups of individuals at Partners—one group getting underage customers kicked out; the other misbehaving & getting kicked out, as well, only to have both groups tussle outside the premises—the press, worldwide, has reported it as a "bias-motivated assault outside a Sea Cliff bar."
This is what needs to be repudiated, whether it is the case or not, or whether it is the one or the other group manipulating the press or not: that is up to the courts to decide. Right now, it appears that the press, more than anyone, needs to have its feet held to the fire. No matter what, Sea Cliff residents need to make a collective, public statement that intolerance and ignorance will not be ignored or tolerated here.

Karin

31 To Karin from John

Karin,

You may not be aware of this but the women who claim to have been attacked outside Partners were previously drinking at a party at Sea Cliff Beach. Apparently the Village allows people to have private parties at the beach and [. . .] caters these events.

John

A neighbor's complaint

Late night scuffles and raucous behavior in and around Partner's seem to be an ongoing problem for the bar's neighbors.

Date: Thu, 13 Sep 2007, 15:13
Subject: sea cliff bar

32 To Karin from Claire (stranger)

Hi Karen

I am a neighbor to Partners, this happens almost every single weekend. This is nothing new, so i'm glad you insist on a protest. This time it became a hate crime, which basically they all are AND the victim will not let it go (as she should not). However, this goes on every weekend and some weeknights (such as last night). The code enforcer is never around and the police when called, in most cases tell the problem makers to "get lost." Last year my husband and I witnessed a gentlemen get his face beat in by 7 men. We called Police, they came and told the guys to get lost and called a ambulence for the poor guy. Next night detectives came to our door. So you see, its ongoing. The Village has to step up to the plate and deal with Partners and Tupelo [a restaurant in the area]. Tupelo has gotten better, however both are hand in hand with sharing clientel after a certain hour. Good luck with your protest! I hope its successful.
Claire

Date: Thu, 13 Sep 2007, 15:25
Subject: sea cliff bar

33 To Claire from Karin

Thanks, Claire. Sorry you have to put up with all that turmoil and ugliness.
Karin

Date: Fri, 14 Sep 2007, 14:40
Subject: sea cliff bar

34 To Karin from Claire

well, thats the price I pay for purchasing this house so many years ago, but I do love it and love living in town, but I hate the night-time horror. I don't know how Sea Cliff lets it go on. All the neighbors feel the same thing. But nothing ever gets done. Sorry I spelt your name wrong on the initial email. I wish you success on Saturday! Hope you have a good turn out. I'll be working till 3.
Claire

Rally postponed

I've acted emotionally and in haste—never optimal conditions for doing things well. I've also missed the news cycles of both local newspapers, which eliminates any chance of publicizing the rally effectively. I suggest to Doug that we postpone the rally from Sept. 15 to the weekend of Sept. 29 (Sept. 22 being Yom Kippur). Two weeks would give us the needed time to do things right. He agrees. I email my contacts the next morning.

Date: Fri, 14 Sep 2007, 09:05
Subject: Rally postponed

35 To 98 contacts

VERY IMPORTANT:

After much deliberation, I have decided it would be best to postpone the rally for tolerance for two weeks to Friday, 9/28 or Saturday, 9/29. It was my hope to organize an appropriate response, as quickly and efficiently as possible, to widespread reports of a bias crime in Sea Cliff and to reaffirm Sea Cliff's long tradition of tolerance. I let my emotions dictate an overhasty response. Better to take the time to organize and publicize a thoughtful, simple and effective event that the entire village can participate in and contribute to. Also, it was never my intent to judge Partners or put them on the spot. I realize now that locating the rally there implies a kind of criticism. Clifton or Memorial Park offers a much more appropriate and generous venue. I welcome your suggestions and participation.
Until then, Karin

Date: Fri, 14 Sep 2007, 09:05
Subject: Sea Cliff rally for tolerance

36 To Karin's 22 SC contacts from Grace, cc: [daughter]

Karen,

Thanks for stepping forward to take action on bias instead of just saying, "How awful!." I will try to join you on the 15th. I would like to know, however, from an eye witness if possible, some more detail about the incident. Do you know why the women and their antagonists were asked to leave and by whom? My view is that there is no excuse for gay bashing whatever the provocation. I would not like to hold Partners responsible, however, for what their customers do outside the bar unless Partners clearly contributed to it. In any case, a demonstration against homophobia is warrented, but I think it is best targeted toward all bigots, both inside and outside the walls of Partners.
Grace

37 To Grace from Karin

Hi Grace,

Thanks for your encouragement. This is a tough thing to do right. The details are conflicting. My purpose has primarily been to respond to the widespread news reports about a bias crime in Sea Cliff and to reaffirm Sea Cliff's long tradition of tolerance. I just postponed the rally for two weeks. In case you didn't get the email here is what I said . . .

Date: Thu 9/13/2007, 7:55 PM
Subject: Sea Cliff rally for tolerance at 6 p.m.

38 To Karin + 25 contacts from Kate

i'm THRILLED that this rally has been organized. unfortunately, many sea cliff residents who would love the opportunity to reaffirm our town's commitment to tolerance will be on a camping trip in montauk this weekend. is there any chance to move the rally to sunday night?
Kate

Date: Fri, 14 Sep 2007, 9:33
Subject: Sea Cliff rally for tolerance at 6 p.m.

39 To Kate from Karin

Hi Kate

Thanks for your response. As it turns out, you're in luck. I've postponed the rally for two weeks.
Karin

Date: Fri, 14 Sep 2007, 09:43
Subject: Sea Cliff rally for tolerance at 6 p.m.

40 To Karin from Kate

Thanks, Karin. I'm very eager to help in whatever way you'd like. It broke my heart to see the news stories about the incident at Partners.
Kate

Different neighbor, same complaint

Apparently the bar is a sore point, but I don't want that to complicate the issue at hand: our community's response to the bias incident. I clarify our purpose to the neighbor.

Date: Fri, 14 Sep 2007, 11:26
Subject: Partners Protest

41 To Karin from Henry

Hi Karin,

I heard about the protest and would like to know what exactly will be taking place on Saturday night. If you could supply some details, I'd appreciate it. I've heard conflicting reports, so I'm not 100% sure it was a hate crime, but I do support protesting the violence and trying to get Partners shut down.

If you don't have time to respond directly, please put me on any mailing list you may have.

Thanks,
Henry

Date: Fri, 14 Sep 2007, 11:47
Subject: Partners Protest

42 To Henry from Karin

Hi Henry,

Thanks for your email. Things are still evolving at this point. We have postponed the rally until 9/28 or 9/29. We will also relocate it to one of the parks. Our purpose is to make a strong unified statement affirming Sea Cliff's tradition of tolerance, in response to the news reports regarding a bias crime in our village. The rally was and is in no way intended as a criticism of Partners.

Here is our latest email: "After much deliberation. . ."
Karin

Date: Fri, 14 Sep 2007, 12:32
Subject: Partners Protest

43 To Karin from Henry

Thanks, Karin. I was actually hoping this would be an opportunity to get Partners shut down. It's a blight on our town. Keep me posted on the event. Do you happen to have the mayor's email address? I would like to write her.

Thanks,
Henry

Reprimand #1

Natalie, a member of an organization whose contact list I had used, writes a group email. In it she takes me to task for my "heinous breech of privacy and misuse of records" in using the contact list. She accuses an "unknown member of the board" of giving me the group's password to access its contact lists and email addresses. Contrary to Natalie's harsh accusation, the addresses were in plain sight for all to see in her recent group email. Because this has nothing to do with the rally and its objectives, I do not argue, but apologize and promise not to do it again.

Date: Fri, 14 Sep 2007, 09:28
Subject: Rally postponed

44 To community organization's contacts from Karin

Dear members,
I apologize for using [the organization's] email addresses. In trying to do the right thing, I apparently did the wrong thing. It was my hope to organize an appropriate response, as quickly and efficiently as possible, to widespread reports of a bias crime in Sea Cliff. When I saw the list of email addresses on [this organization's] recent mailing in my mail box, I thought its members would be a wonderful means of getting the word out. After today's mailing, I will not use the list again.
Karin Barnaby

XIII Reactions to postponement

People take the time to respond and encourage me, some of them strangers. I especially value their support in the wake of my public scolding.

Date: Fri, 14 Sep 2007, 10:42
Subject: Rally postponed

45 To Karin from Eric

Karin
I think your revised plan makes good sense. And I agree that we don't want to judge Partners without knowing exactly what their role was. As we know from the recent experience with the coffee shop, accusations of bias should not be lightly made. What's important is to reaffirm that we are a community that seeks to promote tolerance and acceptance. Good for you for taking up the task of organizing what should be a community-spirited effort.
Eric

46 To Eric from Karin

Thanks, Eric

This is hard and I want to do it right.

Karin

47 To John from Karin

Hi John,

In case you have not heard, we have postponed the rally for two weeks and will relocate it to one of the parks. If you are in touch with the owner/manager of Partners, please forward the message below to them.
Thanks,
Karin

"VERY IMPORTANT:
After much deliberation . . ."

[*John does not respond to this email or any subsequent emails. I run into him at a party some months later and thank him for taking the time and making the effort to challenge me, thus forcing me to clarify my thoughts and purpose.*]

48 To Zoe from Karin

Hi, Zoe,

I thought you'd like to know that we've postponed the rally for two weeks to give us more time to do the right thing and to get the word out. As it stood, we missed the news cycles of both local papers and the thought of no one showing up really distressed me. I've gotten a lot of encouragement and support from good people, who also feel that additional time is necessary. I think we can put on a much more meaningful event in two weeks' time. I'll keep you posted.
I still miss you and Walt very much.
Karin

49 To Karin from Julia

Hi Karin

Just to let you know I totally understand where you were and are coming from. As an over-reactive believer in doing what's right, it is clear that you only meant well. I've written to Natalie and told her how much you and Doug have meant to me by being supportive of my work, and all the people who have performed for the [organization].

Both of you are quite irreplaceable in my opinion. Cheers to you for standing up against the crap! After all Sea Cliff is just as guilty of snobism, racism, and every other kind of ism as every place else.

All best,

Julia

50 To Julia from Karin

Thanks, Julia. Your words of support mean a lot.

See you soon,

Karin

51 To Karin from Bella

Karen,

I think caution and correct information is very important before you determine how to express your outrage. The press coverage has been terrible for Sea Cliff. Allowing more time for organizing a response to "Hate" will also allow more time to get positive press in place.

Bella

52 To Bella from Karin

Thanks, Bella,

It's not easy to do the right thing, but I'm trying.

Karin

53 To Karin from Caroline

Date: Sat, 15 Sep 2007, 11:48
Subject: rally postponed

I understand the haste and I understand the postponement...your heart was in the right place.
All the best,
Caroline

54 To Caroline from Karin

Date: Sat, 15 Sep 2007, 11:55
Subject: rally postponed

Thanks, Caroline. Your understanding and support mean a lot.
Karin

55 To Karin from Caroline

Date: Sat, 15 Sep 2007, 11:59
Subject: Re: rally postponed

I understand because I'm impetuous, and sometimes it doesn't serve me well. I was going to go tonight, as the incident was appalling...but I could see myself doing exactly the same thing... fight while the issue is imminent, or whatever. But, when the fire clears, it's better that it's neutral, away from Partners...and again, it was wonderful for you to respond so quickly. DON'T lose a night's sleep over the [organization] business. Stuff happens.
xo Caroline

56 To Caroline from Karin

Date: Sat, 15 Sep 2007, 12:10
Subject: Thanks

Thanks, again. It's been tumultuous these past days and kind words make all the difference.
Karin

57 To Karin from Lily

Date: Sat. 15 Sep 2007, 12:22
Subject: rally postponed

Karen You don't need to apologize for your response to the gay-bashing incident! Your impulses are generous and ethically right. It is certainly a good idea not to picket Partners, since their involvement in the incident is unproven and unclear.
If the rally takes place on Friday, I'll show up! Will the young woman who was harassed for being gay be there?
Good work!
Lily

58 To Karin from Grace

Karin,

Thanks again for stepping forward. I will watch for info on new date.

Grace

59 To Karin from Sophia

Karin...I think having it in the park is a good idea and I think stressing tolerance of all peoples is a good idea...not just gays...choose a park depending on the crowd you predict..........see you.

Sophia

60 To Karin from Marge

Hi Karin,

It was an honest mistake. I know you meant well. It's such a sad thing that happened. I just hope the right people get punished and the police will be more diligent in the future.

Have a nice weekend,

Marge

61 To Marge from Karin

Hi Marge.

Thanks for your comments. I appreciate them.

Karin

Reprimand #2

Natalie emails me to let me know how much damage my use of the group's contact list has inflicted. She accuses me of causing a board member's resignation. Coincidentally, before the bias incident ever happened, the board member in question had told me that she was "tired" and wanted to step down. According to Natalie, however, it is my fault. Her reasoning, as accurately as I can I paraphrase it here: the board member felt Natalie should not have mentioned my name in the emails she sent to everyone even though my name was on the email everyone received and I, in fact, was the responsible party.

62 To Elaine from Karin

Hi, Elaine,

Is this true?

I am so very sorry and sad if it is.

Karin

Getting it right

Determined to do things right and, given the additional time, I think I should establish a committee. I email individuals who have been supportive to ask for help. For various good reasons they are mostly unavailable. Consequently, Adam remains my only fully engaged co-organizer.

63 To Adam, Kate, Eric, Caroline, Sophia, Gail from Karin

Dear friends,

I would like to have you help me put this rally together. This involves:

1. Picking a date and time: Friday or Saturday evening, 5 or 6 p.m.
2. Determining rally activities. I think they should be very simple: very short, pre-screened statements by anyone who has something relevant to say about tolerance.
3. Publicizing the rally via: a) word of mouth & emails, b) fliers, c) press releases to *Record Pilot*, *GC Gazette*, *Newsday*.

Let me know if you are willing and able.

Thanks,

Karin

64 To Karin from Eric

Karin – [We] are leaving tomorrow. Won't be back till the end of the month. But I just want to tell you that the way you are describing the rally (and location in the park) seems right to me. Hope it comes off well. --

Eric

65 To Karin from Adam

I'm willing and able.---Just wanted to let you know that I had talked to [Village trustee] about posting the rally on the What's New section of the

Sea Cliff website. I am the chair of the website committee and have been putting up events on the website for over two years. Never has any event been restricted. I asked [Village trustee] if the "pro tolerance" rally could be put up and he said he thought it was too political and opinionated. We went back and forth and he asked the mayor and I guess some other "available" trustees and they said they did not want it up on the site. This is really bothering me. I can't believe that our Village government would act to restrict promotion of a community event, regardless of the topic. We have a meeting tomorrow night and I am going to bring it up. What are your thoughts on this? Am I over-reacting? I would just think that with all that has gone on in the Village in the last year that they would welcome a pro-tolerance rally, embrace and put it on the front page of the *Gazette* with their smiling faces. How do you think I should proceed?
Adam

Press release

The press release goes out to local papers and to Newsday *reporters who covered the initial assault story. The* Gold Coast Gazette *publishes the information as submitted. The* Record-Pilot *includes it in a larger article about an arrest in the case.* Newsday *ignores it. I also email it to my contacts, as well as the mayor, whom I'd recently met in town.*

Date: Tue, 18 Sep 2007, 13:13
Subject: Press release - Sea Cliff rally

66 To *Glen Cove Record Pilot, Gold Coast Gazette, Newsday* from Karin

Sea Cliff Rally - Village residents were shocked and saddened to learn of an alleged bias-related assault in Sea Cliff from recent press and TV reports, and from numerous Internet postings. An investigation is underway. Whatever the outcome, village residents feel compelled to repudiate intolerance of any kind, in words or actions, whenever and wherever it is expressed.

Sea Cliff residents will gather for a community-wide rally at Memorial Park to celebrate Sea Cliff's historical commitment to diversity and to reaffirm its unshakeable solidarity with individuals and groups of all backgrounds and persuasions, on Saturday, Sept. 29, 5 p.m., at Memorial Park. For information, call Karin Barnaby.

67 To Adam, Doug, Kate, Eric, Caroline, Gail, Zoe, Mayor from Karin

I thought you'd like to see the press release I sent out to appear in this week's papers. I'll follow up next week with more details.
Karin

"Sea Cliff Rally - Village residents were shocked and saddened . . ."

68 To Karin from Adam

Great work!
Peace and Pay it Forward,
Adam

69 To Karin from Gail

Hi Karin,
The press release is very good - just the right tone.
Do you want me to forward it to my Sea Cliff group email addresses?
Gail

70 To Gail from Karin

Thanks, Gail. That would be great. If you want to solicit statements, poems, songs, whatever, that might be good, too. People need to submit their contributions to you/us ahead of time, just to be sure we maintain the positive, affirmative tone. I think this is a real opportunity to do something good.
Karin

71 To Karin from Adam

Went to the website committee meeting tonight and [trustee] said that he, the other trustees and the mayor re-visited the notion of posting info about the rally on the what's new section of the Sea Cliff website.

They basically are willing to post a pro-tolerance rally announcement, but nothing linking it to the incident. Pretty much the second half of your press release and not the first. They said that I should email them what we want posted and they will review it. I made it clear that this was my issue and that I was pretty sure you could care less if it was posted on the website. Have any thoughts?
Adam

Date: Tue, 18 Sep 2007, 21:35
Subject: press release - Sea Cliff rally

72 To Adam from Karin

I spoke with the mayor today re. our plans & she brought up the notion of posting something on the website. I also forwarded the press release to her. So, I'm not sure if she spoke with [Village trustee] & website committee members or plans to. I'll gladly leave it up to you to handle it in any way you think is right.
Thanks,
Karin

Date: Thu, 20 Sep 2007, 11:37
Subject: Sea Cliff Rally

73 To Karin from Elaine

Karin,
This Rally looks good--very appropriate and positive. I will forward your letter, starting with my husband!
Elaine

Date: Fri, 21 Sep 2007, 10:43
Subject: press release - Sea Cliff rally

74 To Karin from Sophia

I think your press release is wonderful!!! Thank you..............Sophia
(We just got back from a mini vacation in New Hampshire....fun)

An arrest

One of the local papers, the Glen Cove Record-Pilot, *headlines the news of the arrest of a young homeless man from out of state in the bias assault. The article incorporates our press release about the Sea Cliff rally into the* Record-Pilot's *own statement about residents "outraged by the hate crime." This makes it seem like it is my statement, which it is not. This is unfortunate because I'd resolved to avoid all negative or judgmental opinions.*

GLEN COVE RECORD PILOT

Arrest Made in Sea Cliff Bar Bias Attack -Village Residents to Rally Against Intolerance by Lyne Antonaccio

SEA CLIFF, September 21, 2007 - According to Lt. Albert Anderson of the Nassau County Police Department's Sixth Squad, the police have arrested a homeless man for a bias-related robbery of a former Top Chef television program contender and three other women outside the bar Partners in Sea Cliff the night of Sept. 1.

Matthew W. Walli, 20, of Oregon, was arrested on Sept. 12 and charged with second-degree robbery as a bias crime. Police said Mr. Walli was part of a group of approximately 12 people who confronted Josie Smith-Malave, a competitor on the second season of Bravo's Top Chef and a Brooklyn resident, and her friends after they were ejected from the bar.

"There has been one arrest, which is great. It's the first of what I hope to be many more," said Yetta Kurland, Ms. Smith-Malave's attorney. "There were between nine and 12 attackers. I very much am hoping there will be additional arrests in the near future and this matter will continue to be treated as a bias crime."

Ms. Smith-Malave said she and her friends made the trip to Long Island over Labor Day weekend for a friend's birthday party in Sea Cliff. Around 11 p.m. on Sept. 1, she said, they walked to Partners on Sea Cliff Ave. Shortly after ordering drinks, the women were asked to leave the bar. Ms. Smith-Malave, who is openly gay, said they were asked to leave because members of her group, who were all over 21, looked underage and had not been proofed by the bouncer when entering the bar. However, other members of her group were told they were asked to leave because two women were dancing together and it was getting "too gay," Ms. Kurland said.

They were followed outside by a group of young adults who made derogatory comments regarding the women's sexual orientation, as well as spitting on them several times and throwing sticks, cups and other objects at them, Ms. Kurland stated. Several members of the group of attackers, both male and female, then physically attacked the women, said the attorney, kicking and punching them. Mr. Walli allegedly also stole Ms. Smith-Malave's video camera, which she had been using to tape the assault, the attorney added.

While the attack occurred, patrons at the bar and others on the street laughed and took pictures while watching, according to Ms. Smith-Malave.

Nassau County Police Department made no arrests at the time, according to a police report and none of the women, who suffered minor bruises and lacerations, went to the hospital.

The day after the incident, said Ms. Kurland, after destroying the video footage, Mr. Walli returned the camera to Partners. Partners contacted the police, giving them Walli's name. The investigation is ongoing, according to Lt. Anderson.

"Underage drinking and bias-related violence should simply not be tolerated, and even more concerning is the fact that the bar, the patrons, and the officers who initially responded turned a deaf ear to the senseless attack on these women," said Ms. Kurland. "This incident constitutes not only bias-related violence under New York State hate crime laws, but gang assault in the second degree, a Class C Felony, which carries with it substantial penalties. These are serious crimes and we take them very seriously."

She added, "Initially, police were not as responsive as they should have been, but after our Sept. 12 press conference, local authorities and the [Nassau County] District Attorney's office have been responsive to our request to continue to treat this as a serious, bias crime and as a gang assault. ... This [incident] is clearly an example of why we have hate crime legislation [and] how out-of-control gangs in any neighborhood can become abusive and unstoppable when alcohol and ignorance are combined."

Residents of Sea Cliff, many outraged by the hate crime, are taking matters into their own hands with a community-wide rally at Memorial Park on Saturday, Sept. 29 at 5 p.m. "Village residents were shocked and saddened to learn of [the] assault," said Karin Barnaby, who helped organize the event. "An investigation is underway. Whatever the outcome, village residents feel compelled to repudiate intolerance of any kind, in words or actions, whenever and wherever it is expressed. Sea Cliff residents will gather for a community-wide rally to celebrate Sea Cliff's historical commitment to diversity and to reaffirm its unshakeable solidarity with individuals and groups of all backgrounds and persuasions." Owners of Partners were not available for comment.

Reprinted with permission from Anton Community Newspapers

The Human Rights Campaign

Sarah, an organizer with the Human Rights Campaign and not a Sea Cliff resident, responds to our press release with a phone call and offer to help spread the word to other organizations. This would expand our outreach. I had been so focused on Sea Cliff that it had not occurred to me to appeal to rights organizations or to the larger Long Island community.

Date: Fri, 21 Sep 2007, 11:49
Subject: Sea Cliff rally

75 To Sarah from Karin

Hi Sarah,

It was so good to talk with you. Here's the press release for you to distribute. It would be great if you can get the word out.

Thanks,

Karin

Date: Fri, 21 Sep 2007, 12:57
Subject: Sea Cliff rally

76 To Karin from Sarah

Thank you. I will start to circulate, and encourage other group leaders to contact you if they have any questions. I will most likely submit a paragraph on behalf of the Human Rights Campaign.

Thank you again for your local leadership on this issue. I am looking forward to meeting you. My home address is [. . .] Glen Cove.

Sarah

Rally opposition

Bob, a village resident, opposes the rally. He emails all my contacts, urging them "not to participate in any gathering, rally, organized march, or other such named event planned for this Saturday in support of the bias assault that occurred on September 1, in the Village. [. . .] Let's stay neutral, [. . .] Sea Cliff does not need this kind of publicity! whether you are ANTI gay or Pro gay... it does not matter. It only adds fuel to the fire." He encourages residents to "call the police department and urge them to do more to find all the others involved and to charge them." I cannot understand his opposition. Especially distressing to me is his observation, "After all the individual arrested is not a resident, just another visitor passing through." How convenient to have the one outsider, among a dozen or so local young people, take the rap.

77 To Gail from Lee

Sent: Friday, September 21, 2007 3:51
Subject: Fwd: pro rally gathering this Saturday

To Gail
this just gets more and more interesting! So now there's a rally "in support of the bias assault" according to this email? Who is this Bob? Curious!
I think I'll write him back now about this....
Lee (acquaintance)

Date: Fri, 21 Sep 2007, 16:19
Subject: Fwd: pro rally gathering this Saturday

78 To Adam from Karin

Hi, Adam,
I see from Bob's email list that you received his email, as well. Not sure what to make of it. It makes no sense. I heard from Chuck Lavine [NYS Assemblyman] yesterday who said he would come if he didn't have to be in Oregon that day. He was very supportive. Sarah wants to participate by making a brief statement for the Human Rights Campaign. She said you know each other. That's it so far. I'll try to put a flier together today or tomorrow. I guess this weekend would be a good time to post them around town. Also, I think we need some means of amplification . . . in case more than a handful show up.
Talk to you soon.
Karin

Date: Fri, 21 Sep 2007, 20:54
Subject: Fwd: pro rally gathering this Saturday

79 To Karin from Adam

I have a pa system we could use. Just need a place to plug in. I can put up fliers sat morning. Forget Bob.
Peace, Adam

Date: Fri, 21 Sep 2007, 21:30
Subject: PA system

80 To Adam from Karin

PA system sounds good. I think there are some sort of outlets in the park since all those musicians do concerts there. I'm applying for a permit to use the park on Monday. Talked to [village official] about it. I'll find out about the outlets then.
Karin

81 To Adam from Karin

Hi Adam

I've attached a draft of the flier. Let me know what you think. If it's OK, I'll run some off tomorrow morning. How many should we do?

Karin

Publicity Flier

---

tolerance fairness humanity empathy love
open-mindedness generosity friendship
kindness understanding community diversity

tolerance

community

Sea Cliff

Join us
Saturday, Sept. 29,
5 p.m. Memorial Park
Info: Karin Barnaby

tolerance fairness humanity empathy love
open-mindedness generosity friendship
kindness understanding community diversity

82 To Karin from Adam

How dare you stand up for all those things in the flier. You are
obviously a trouble maker ;-)
I don't understand how it is that some people don't get this and resist it.
Anyway, the flier looks great. I'm not sure where you want to put the
fliers. If it's just Sea Cliff and Roslyn Aves I would say maybe 30, but if
you want to include the CVS shopping center, North Shore Farms and
stores up and down Glen Cove Avenue. I would maybe make about 100.
(You can post more than one per store). Color copies can get expensive.
I think they are about $1 a piece. I can contribute some dough if you'd
like or you may want to see if someone like Printstars in the Dunkin
Donut's shopping center will just donate them.
Either way, the flier looks great.
If we bring the PA would we need a permit, or do you think they'd let it
slide?
Would you like me to contact [County Legislator]?
--Also, I have a meeting at 10 at Village Hall. It should probably end
around 11:30. Will you be around then. Maybe I could stop by and pick
up some of the fliers?
Let me know.
Adam
Peace and Pay it Forward,

A puzzling insinuation

*Marilyn, a stranger, questions my claim about Sea Cliff's "historical
commitment to diversity," without mentioning specifics. I don't know what to
make of her vague insinuations, but they disturb me. I ask her to explain, but
she does not reply for several weeks, not until after the rally is over. I include
her eventual response here.*

83 To Karin from Marilyn

Hello Karin,
We received the e-mail informing us of the gathering to affirm Sea Cliff's
residents' commitment to support diversity and condemn the recent
altercation at the local bar on Sea Cliff Avenue, Partners. Do you think

that this call to meeting is motivated by how we see ourselves to be, or perhaps, how we want to be perceived by the outside world?

I pose this question because of the statement included in the e-mail I received which attests to the historical commitment to diversity which supposedly defines Sea Cliff.

Ted and I love the village, our children and grandchildren live here, but you and we know the historical record of the village would make one more reticent about using terminology such as "historical commitment to diversity."

Sincerely,

Marilyn

Date: Sat, 22 Sep 2007, 18:32
Subject: Sea Cliff

84 To Marilyn from Karin

Hi Marilyn,

I don't understand what you mean by "the historical record of the village." I've lived here for 40 years and have experienced an extraordinary openness to and tolerance of diversity, non-conformity, creativity, eccentricity. When my husband and I mention that we live in Sea Cliff to people in other communities, they often remark on its "Bohemian," artistic character. One person said, "Oh, Sea Cliff. That's where all the wackos are." Maybe I've just had different experiences, but let me know if and how I may be wrong.

Karin

Date: Sun, 30 Sep 2007, 23:39
Subject: Re: Sea Cliff

85 To Karin from Marilyn

Dear Karin,

In response to the question you posed of whether I believed you were wrong in your statement about Sea Cliff being a historically tolerant and inclusive community, I reply that, no one is always right and, of course, no-one is always wrong and we should therefore shy away from broad, general statements that encompass an undefined span of time in reference to this topic.

My family and I moved to Sea Cliff twenty-six years ago, so, as the tradition goes, we can now be considered "Sea Cliffers," but I remember the time, twenty-six years ago, when our neighbors viewed us as the "unwelcomed minorities." The B--s residing at Dubois Avenue asked me as we were moving in, "How many of you are there?" The name of M-- might have set off a red flag signaling we were Jewish even though we were Italian. I don't know if being Italian at that time would have made much difference

Our friends then, the F--s, had their own story to tell.

You say that when you mention Sea Cliff to folks from other communities they now identify Sea Cliff as a community of "Bohemians" and perhaps, as one person said to you: "Wackos." Well, I certainly think that it can't hurt Sea Cliff to be known as a community of artists but be aware, one more time, of the stereotypes people attach to people who engage in the arts.

On a different note, today I bought a print from your husband at the Sea Cliff MiniMart. I admired his watercolors when they were exhibited at the Daniel Gale Agency on Sea Cliff Avenue and am now the happy and proud owner of one of his prints. He is a fine artist and a very humble one at that.

Thanks for responding to my original e-mail,

Marilyn

The kindness of strangers

The Smiths, whom I don't know, respond to Bob's attempt to discourage people from attending the rally. Their poignant yet pointed commentary lays out what is at stake when a community ignores acts of bias in its midst. Their evocation of a Montana town's enlightened response to a bias crime is inspiring. The Smith's thoughtfulness and words are a deeply appreciated gift.

Date: Sat, 22 Sep 2007, 17:15
Subject: Re: Compelled to write

86 To Bob from the Smiths, cc: Bob's contact list

Bob, I thank you for the comments you wrote to me about the rally. I feel compelled to respond, especially the part where you state:

"Sea Cliff does not need this kind of publicity ! whether you are ANTI gay or Pro gay... it does not matter. the final result is that Sea Cliff as a community does not need this kind of exposure. It does not help... all that it does is add more fuel to the fire, at a time when it is finally starting to die down. If you hold a function for either side of the issue, the Village becomes marked as having an official opinion, which may cause the other side to want a function also. WE (the Village of Sea Cliff as a whole) do not need to be thought of in this light as being on either side. Lets stay neutral !! After all the individual arrested is not a resident, just another visitor passing through."

The letter reminded me of the story of a famous German pastor named

Martin Niemoller who wrote the following:

"First they came for the Jews
and I did not speak out
because I was not a Jew.
Then they came for the Communists
and I did not speak out
because I was not a Communist.
Then they came for the trade unionists
and I did not speak out
because I was not a trade unionist.
Then they came for me
and there was no one left
to speak out for me."
    Pastor Martin Niemöller

I'm not sure people view this as a pro gay-rally as much of a statement against people who hate. The bottom line is our town in most people's opinion (wrongfully) is portrayed as a town that had a group of people from a local bar beat up a woman, use vile language against her, and steal her belongings, all because of her sexual orientation. Clearly, we are not a community that condones this ... Not too long ago in Billings, Montana there was an incident where someone threw a brick at a menorah in a window, shattering glass all over a child's room. The family, one of the few Jewish families in town, was frightened and concerned that this may be how the entire town viewed them. The investigating police officer gave the family advice that maybe they should not put the menorah back in the window. The town rallied the next day and all the townspeople, some six thousand strong, cut out cardboard menorahs and put them in their windows, even though they themselves were not Jewish. The town was not concerned that this may bring a rally of ANTI Jews to the town and only make things worse, but thought that supporting this family that lived in their community was the right thing to do. It is clear that there are gay people in our community. They are our friends and neighbors, they raise their children here, work here and are part of our community. They deserve for us to stand behind them as a community not in the shadows because of fear that others who are ANTI-GAY may come here and march. Some may think using the Jews and the persecution of them is an unfair comparison. If a person in one of our local places of business was beaten up, spoken to with vile racist language, chased and had their property stolen because of their skin color or religion, I believe we as a community should do something. This incident, in my opinion, is no different. I understand from your letter that you will not be at the rally because you are fearful that others may come who hate the people who were persecuted in our town. In my opinion, I'm not sure that's the stance I want to teach my children. If, after the rally, a group of people comes to Sea Cliff for an anti-gay rally then I guess we as a community must face them. Not doing anything due to the fear of them coming to our town is exactly what Pastor Niemoller was talking about in his famous saying. The good people in our town are looking to see what we as a Sea Cliff community are made of. I say we put our menorahs in the window (so to speak) and show that we as a community welcome everyone regardless of color, religion or sexual orientation.

Community and individuality are not opposites, you must rally with the oppressed and hated. (attached is a picture of the town of Billings Montana marching though the streets with menorahs)
the Smiths

Date: Tue, 25 Sep 2007, 11:40
Subject: Compelled to write

87 To the Smiths from Karin
Hi Smiths.
I want to tell you what a fine response you wrote to Bob. Thank you for doing that. It means a lot to hear you speak up in such a thoughtful and constructive way about why doing the right thing is essential.
Thanks again,
Karin

Date: Wed, 26 Sep 2007, 16:16
Subject: Compelled to write

88 To Karin from the Smiths
Thanks for the kind words...
The Smiths

The perspective of the gay and lesbian community
Angela from the Long Island Lesbian Cancer Initiative (LILCI), informed about the Sea Cliff rally by Sarah (Human Rights Campaign), offers a hitherto missing perspective: the thoughts and feelings of the lesbian and gay community. The assault, in her words, "sent shock waves beyond Sea Cliff." Her email hits home how important it is for the Sea Cliff community to not remain silent, but to speak up against this bias incident.

89 To Karin from Angela, cc: Sarah [Human Rights Campaign]

Hi Karin,

As per my conversation with Sarah, I'd like to introduce myself and offer to be of service in preparing for the upcoming rally.

Prior to your press release, the local sexual minority women's community had begun planning a visible community action to condemn violence and intolerance. Our goal was to identify a safe space and create an opportunity for community members and allies to gather in peaceful solidarity, regardless of the outcome of the NCPD [Nassau County Police Dept.] effort. A community chorus was asked if they would sing and a number of gay and lesbian affirming congregations were asked if they'd provide an invocation (if that's the right word). Groups from NOW and BiasHelp to Pride For Youth (Nassau County's gay and lesbian youth center) were engaged and ready to respond once a day/time/location could be set.

What an incredible moment it was to read your press release. Personally, I recalled the multiple rejections Long Island's gay and lesbian communities faced while requesting permits for a rally and march for gay civil rights on Long Island (now the Long Island Pride Parade). I think it was about 13 or 14 years ago that the first rally and march took place in Huntington. That effort took a lawsuit to secure an event permit and the first few years, businesses shut their doors. Huntington has come a long way since then – as have we all. By organizing this community action, the Village of Sea Cliff's response to this bias incident sends an incredibly powerful message that Sea Cliff is one, unified and diverse, multicultural community and that bias on its streets or against any of its citizens is not ok.

In addition to this incident's impact on Sea Cliff's culturally diverse citizens, this incident's impact sent shock waves beyond Sea Cliff, to sexual minority women throughout Nassau County. My ask is that you keep in mind the far reaching extent of this incident and that you kindly allow these women's voices to be represented and engaged in the community response on the 29th. I ask for your advisement on how we can achieve our mutual goals in coalition rather than the redundancy of organizing two separate rallys.

I am out of town at a conference (don't feel bad for me, it's in Puerto Rico this year!) but through the wonders of cell phones and blackberrys,

I am as accessible as if I were home on Long Island. My cell phone number . . . and this email goes to my Blackberry. I look forward to hearing from you.
Onward,
Angela, (LILCI)

90 To Angela from Karin

Hi Angela,
It was so good to hear from you. This is a fairly unstructured event that aspires to make a statement about tolerance in general and is not limited to gay issues. We welcome participation in the form of short pertinent statements, poems, songs, etc. which should be submitted to me in writing by Thursday, Sept. 27. I insist on screening contributions because we want to ensure an upbeat, positive event.
So far: I will read a statement. Two other individuals have said they would, too. Two Middle School students want to sing the Beatles "Let it be" and Lennon's "Imagine." I have not invited any public officials because I want everyone to decide on their own whether or not to participate. So far, [NYS Assemblyman] has called to say he would have participated if he didn't have to be in Oregon next weekend. Sarah said she would talk to [Nassau County legislator]. As you can see, there is much that is unforeseeable here, including how many people will show up.
I look forward to hearing from you,
Karin

91 To Adam from Karin

Hi Adam,
Just received this email [from Angela] & thought it would interest you. It makes a powerful case for our rally. Here's my response, as well.
Karin

Courage and tolerance

Adam runs a draft of his statement by me. Thoughtful and to the point, he offers a definition of tolerance that perfectly argues for the kind of community action we are organizing.

92 To Karin from Adam

Hey Karin, here is what I wrote up. What do you think?

"The late Reverend Ralph W. Sockman once said "The test of courage comes when we are in the minority. The test of tolerance comes when we are in the majority."

Some of us have come here to Sea Cliff's Memorial Park because we are tolerant. Some of us have come here because we are courageous. Some of us have come here because we are both.

It is clear, however, that all of us who have come here believe in one thing: the complete and utter acceptance of people of all nationalities, ethnicities, races, genders and sexual orientation.

We do not fear difference, but celebrate it. We did not silence diversity, but offer it a chance to speak. We do not demand uniformity from variance, but encourage divergent thinkers and independent minds.

We welcome all individuals and are proud to do so. Here at Memorial Park, the citizens of Sea Cliff and the community at large should remember what we stand for: Peace, justice, acceptance and equality for all."

Peace and Pay it Forward,
Adam

93 To Adam from Karin

I LOVE it. It's perfect. I was thinking about the minority/majority dynamic yesterday and realized how important it really was/is that non-gays champion gay rights. That's the real test of democracy. So glad you said it so much better.

One typo: "We *did* not silence diversity . . ." I think you want to say "We *do* not silence diversity . . ."

We should probably try out your PA system one day this week & make sure it works.

Thanks again,
Karin

Organizational details
Fliers, permissions, PA system, getting the word out, confirming participants.

Date: Sat, 22 Sep 2007, 17:17
Subject: Sea Cliff rally

94 To Sarah from Karin
I look forward to receiving your Human Rights Campaign statement. I'm attaching the flier if you want to distribute any.
Karin

Date: Sat, 22 Sep 2007, 20:30
Subject: flier

95 To 34 SC contacts from Karin
Hello again. I've attached copies of the flier—one black and white and one in color. If you could forward it or print and distribute it as best you can, that would be good.
Thanks,
Karin

Date: Sat, 22 Sep 2007, 20:38
Subject: fliers

96 To Adam from Karin
Adam, I dropped an envelope containing fliers off at your house, btw. your front doors.
Thanks for your offer, but I had a $25 coupon for Staples which paid for almost all of the printing. Sarah said she would be meeting with [County Legislator] this week & would mention it to her. FYI I have not and will not invite anyone to participate, including our trustees and the mayor, beyond the general invitation already extended via email & press release. People have to feel the need to join us and/or speak all on their own.
Karin

Date: Sun, 23 Sep 2007, 08:59
Subject: fliers

97 To Karin from Adam
Hey Karin, just got home and saw the fliers. Nice job. The only thing is your email address says "yaoo.com" instead of "yahoo.com." I'm not sure if you care and I'm sure most people would be able to figure out the mistake, but I just wanted to check with you before I put them up.
Peace and Pay it Forward,
Adam

98 To Karin from Lily

Karin, as it turns out I saw Tony and Ben [a gay couple in town] today and I gave them that flyer. They are sure to give it to many of their friends....
Lily

99 To Lily from Karin

Great. Thanks, Lily.
Karin

100 To Angela, Sarah, Audrey, and 15 additional SC contacts, from Karin

Hi everyone,

First: my apologies to those of you who have already gotten this information. Please help spread the word about this Saturday's rally for tolerance. Below is the text of my press release and I'm attaching the flier. Any way that you can help would be great.
Thanks,
Karin

101 From Anonymous to Karin

I am saddened and shocked that people are compelled to act on something that they don't know anything about. I wouldn't participate in something like this if they paid me. Maybe they should find out the facts before they participate.

[The disparaging tone of this anonymous email is obviously intended to insult me, but I'm not sure what's being insinuated or to what purpose.]

102 To Mary from Angela, CC: 9 contacts

Good morning all,

Thank you for your emails.

My ask is if chapter leadership would consider speaking, even briefly, to be the voice of feminism on tolerance and nonviolence. Statements, poems, songs whatever is presented needs to be pre-screened by Karin Barnaby by Thursday, Sept 27th.

I am at a conference, returning on Sunday, Sept 30 (don't feel bad for me, the meeting is in sunny Puerto Rico !!). It's a crazy busy week of meetings from 7am with networking every evening till 9pm . I'm also preparing for a presentation to the Board of Directors tomorrow and facilitating a round table discussion later in the week. I sincerely apologize for missing this very important program and a chapter meeting, and in asking for a presence from NOW while I'm going to be absent. The context that concerns me and the reason I feel it is so important for a visible NOW presence is that a number of groups who themselves have been targets of intolerance (mostly Jewish groups who have experienced anti-Semitic graffiti and have also worked with BiasHelp – Long Island's anti-violence organization) have declined their invitation to stand in solidarity at this rally because of the gay factor of the incident. As the voice for equality for all women and a leader against violence against women, NOW's visibility is needed even more because many others – even those with personal experience with hate and bias - will not stand in solidarity (I love those big NOW logo discs because they are *so* visible!). My only ask is that whoever speaks specifically articulates "sexual minority women" for 3 reasons: sexual minority women are an invisible population unless specifically mentioned, sexual minority women use different language to describe themselves so it is impossible to be inclusive simply by using the term "lesbian" or "homosexual" (i.e. some may call themselves: queer, lesbian, gay woman, bisexual, polysexual or pansexual and the list goes on), lastly, in a situation like this it is extremely empowering to hear "allies" speak in solidarity (these are people who don't identify as gay or lesbian).

In the mean time, I am circulating the attachment Mary just forwarded about the Sept meeting under separate cover to my list with a personal invitation to participate.

And finally – Nora, Mary, Julia - My personal and most sincere appreciation for your mentorship and solidarity. Your kind and thoughtful responses during this process (and by that I mean taking the time and putting critical consideration and thought into your advisement) has been the fuel for my action, planning and engagement rather than inaction, apathy or retreat. It is truly a privilege to work among you.
Warmly,
Angela

Disappointment

Two boys, who had volunteered to perform John Lennon's "Imagine" and the Beatles' "Let It Be" at the rally, are unable to do so because they have a baseball game. Young people's participation in our rally is not only an important social and generational statement, but their particular musical selections would add a compelling musical-philosophical touch.
This is a huge disappointment.

Date: Mon, 24 Sep 2007, 10:44
Subject: Sea Cliff rally

103 To Karin from Helene

Karin. As it turns out, we will not be unable to attend the rally on Saturday. [The boys] have a baseball game. I will, however, continue to spread the word.
Peace,
Helene

Date: Mon, 24 Sep 2007, 11:37
Subject: Sea Cliff rally

104 To Helene from Karin

Hi Helene,

I'm very disappointed. The boys' contribution would have added just the right touch. Are you sure? Don't they play baseball earlier in the afternoon? If you should get back in time, please know that the boys are welcome to participate.
Thanks,
Karin

Date: Mon, 24 Sep 2007, 12:04
Subject: Sea Cliff rally

105 To Karin from Helene

The boys are playing a double-header beginning at 1pm. It's not likely they'll finish in time to make the Rally, but we could try.
Helene

106 To Helene from Karin

Can't do more than that. If at all possible, it would be great, even if they could make it in time to perform at the end. It would provide a memorable closure to the event. I would hate to lose the simple beauty of two young people expressing themselves via the Beatles' thoughtful, lyrical sensibility.

Thanks.

Karin

Participant #1: the Sea Cliff Methodist Church

Constance, a friend, calls to say that members of the Sea Cliff Methodist Church would like to participate in the rally. They are and will remain the only Sea Cliff church or organization to do so. I am very encouraged and grateful. I email her a press release and flier.

Date: Mon, 24 Sep 2007, 14:17
Subject: SC press release & flier

107 To Karin from Constance

Karin, it all [press release & flier] came out very well. I will type the statement that is on our Sunday Bulletin every week:

"The Mission of the United Methodist Church of Sea Cliff is to carry out God's purposes as defined for us by the life of Jesus Christ. As His disciples we seek to reach out to our own community and the world to support God's work and to invite, without exclusion, all people to a life of love and service in Jesus' name. We pray that your time with us will be a joyful celebration of life and faith."

Below this is printed:

"Open Hearts, Open Minds, Open Doors"
The People of the United Methodist Church
Until we talk again,
Constance

Participant #2: NOW (National Organization for Women)

In response to Angela's appeal, Mary, active with the National Organization for Women (NOW) comes aboard.

Date: Mon, 24 Sep 2007, 14:00
Subject: Rally

108 To Angela from Mary, CC: Karin + 8 contacts

Okay, Angela --What I take from this is that there is no FOCUS -- meaning we are not rallying or demonstrating AGAINST anyone or any group/municipality/business, etc.

I will be glad to bring the NOW ROUNDS. I will submit a 5-line poem I wrote in 1990 -- entitled Love Thy Neighbor or Tolerance 101. Karin Barnaby can decide whether it is appropriate.

I will ask Karin for the exact location, corner, place in Sea Cliff, and how to get there. I take it then, that you will not be at our 9/29 meeting at Stony Brook -- Enjoy yourself and tell us all about it when you get back.

Om

Mary

Date: Mon, 24 Sep 2007, 14:12
Subject: SEA CLIFF GATHERING IN RESPONSE TO THE LESBIAN BIAS INCIDENT

109 To Karin from Mary

Hello, Karin,

I'm responding to Angela's call for participation in your event this coming Saturday in Sea Cliff -- I need directions to the exact spot, corner, place where this will take place - and the time. Herewith is a very short poem I wrote in 1990 - during a hateful period of race bias -- if you are old enough, perhaps you will remember it - a black man had the misfortune of walking through the Bensonhurst neighborhood in Brooklyn -- and was chased to his death --

Love Thy Neighbor

or

Tolerance 101

Red headlines tell the tale of Yusuf Hawkins,
victim of the word made manifest.
I fear the hate that flickered like a flame that night,
igniting other coiled pockets of hate
as it flashed its way to death.

I look forward to your response.

In Sisterhood,

Mary

Date: Mon, 24 Sep 2007, 14:16
Subject: SEA CLIFF RALLY - 9/29

110 To Mary from Karin

Hi, Mary,

Yes, I do remember Yusuf Hawkins and I am old enough. Your poem is great. Definitely read it on Saturday. The rally will take place in Memorial Park at the western end of Sea Cliff Avenue at 5 p.m. I look forward to

seeing you there. You are more than welcome to say a few words. Please be good enough to submit your contribution to me by Thursday. I don't know what the NOW Rounds are. Please enlighten me.
Thanks.
Karin

Date: Mon, 24 Sep 2007, 17:03
Subject: SEA CLIFF RALLY - 9/29

111 To Karin from Mary

The NOW ROUNDS -- are the NOW logo -- National Organization for Women which we use for identification when we have meetings.
Mary

Date: Mon, 24 Sep 2007, 18:53
Subject: SEA CLIFF RALLY - 9/29

112 To Mary from Karin

Thanks, Mary. Are you planning on distributing the NOW Rounds? I had hoped to keep this rally fairly general and apolitical while focusing fully on tolerance/intolerance.
Karin

Date: Mon, 24 Sep 2007, 18:31
Subject: flier

113 To 23 contacts from Grace, CC: a relative

Thanks, Karin, for doing the careful, thoughtful, time-consuming legwork. I'll be there.
Grace

Date: Mon, 24 Sep 2007, 17:20
Subject: SC flier

114 To Karin from Sarah, Human Rights Campaign

Thanks, Karin. I will circulate at our monthly cocktail event on Wed at RS Jones in Merrick.
Sarah

[*The above is one of the occasional emails Sarah sends me, but I can never quite pin her down regarding if and how she plans to participate. No matter what, I am enormously grateful to her for establishing the contact with Angela and, through her, to all the other participants.*]

Date: Mon, 24 Sep 2007, 19:05
Subject: flier

115 To Zoe from Karin

Hi Zoe,
I'm not sure if I sent you a copy of the flier or not. But here it is (again?) in case. I've been juggling a lot of email & have gotten a lot of

encouraging feedback. Looks like we're going to have something good happening in SC on Saturday.
Keep the faith, as our dear Isabel likes to say.
Karin

Date: Tue, 25 Sep 2007, 07:54
Subject: flier

116 To Karin from Zoe
So colorful, positive, and alluring. I'll send good energy from nearby: we'll be in the city seeing *Wicked* and having dinner with our kids.

A cautious Village Board
I'd expected and hoped that the mayor and trustees would want to participate in the rally, but have not heard from them. Their decision to not post rally information on the Village website sends a disappointing message. I am sorry for their official caution (?) and/or discomfort (?).

Date: Tue, 25 Sep 2007, 13:04
Subject: rally

117 To Karin from Adam
The board is Wimpy. Overheard people making fun of the rally this morning. Also got an email asking if it was a poetry reading. Very disappointed in the mayor and the trustees response. How could they not post it? I want to know who voted for/against it.

------Original Message------

Sent: Sep 25, 2007 7:37 AM
Subject: rally

To: Adam from Trustee [forward to Karin]
Adam, after considerable discussion the Board of Trustees decided not to promote the rally on the website. It was a split vote.
The BOT did approve a request for use of Memorial Park for the rally and a permit will be issued.

Date: Tue, 25 Sep 2007, 10:37
Subject: rally

118 To Adam from Karin
Adam,
Don't give it another thought. People do so little thinking and so much assuming. They have already decided what they want to decide. I am amazed about some of the comments, all anonymous, relayed to me by Gail as "some people's concerns," first thing this morning. Not sure why she did that.

The response generally has been overwhelmingly supportive in any case. Every store in SC gladly put up the flier. The two boys who were going to sing "Let It Be" and "Imagine" turn out to have a baseball double header that afternoon & might not be able to make it. I would like to have someone sing those songs. Any ideas? I'm going to ask around. So far, it's you and I and reps from NOW and the Methodist Church who are planning to say something. Let's see what else comes in.
Thanks, again, Adam.
Karin

Bob's score sheet: 71 agree, 6 disagree, 7 undecided

Date: Tue, 25 Sep 2007, 20:00

Bob, who, in a previous email, urged people not to attend the rally, sends an update, his own rough survey of residents' opinions. According to him, most people agree with him. It's not really clear what they agree with, but I assume it is with his vague clichés about staying "neutral" and not needing "this kind of publicity." Last but not least, he says two people are "TOTALLY FOR IT and referred to it as a GAY ASSEMBLY." Also, Newsday apparently contacted him. He says: "After telling [the reporter] the whole story I am happy to say, that he also agrees that there is no news worthy story here, so he will not be coming out."

A second press release
Bob's email makes me rethink the need for a follow-up press release and appeal for support. Adam agrees.

Date: Tue, 25 Sep 2007, 22:41
Subject: This week's papers

119 To Karin from Adam
Is the rally going to be in this week's papers?
Bob is really making my blood boil. Obviously, tolerance is way too controversial. What did Gail say to you? Do you have any estimate of how many people are going to show? I know it's hard, but even a guestimate?
Peace and Pay it Forward,
Adam

Date: Wed, 26 Sep 2007, 07:25
Subject: SC rally

120 To the Editors of *Glen Cove Record Pilot, Gold Coast Gazette*
If at all possible & if it's not too late, could you include the attached in

this week's paper? As a box? As an ad--1/8 or 1/4 page, depending on the cost? I was not going to submit anything because the word is out, but there is a movement afoot to discourage people from attending. I don't know if you are aware of that. If not, I'll gladly forward the emails. I'll give you a call later.
Thanks,
Karin

Ad

Date: **Wed, 26 Sep 2007, 08:03**
Subject: This week's papers

121 To Adam from Karin

I wasn't going to put anything in because the word is out. But I sent both papers a reworked flier (attached) to include as a box or as an ad. I don't know what to expect on Saturday. Whatever happens is fine. It will be a good gauge of what's really going on in Sea Cliff. I think Thurs into Fri we'll get a better sense of things. I almost want to forward Bob's emails to *Newsday*. I did let the local editors know that there was an effort afoot to discourage attendance at the rally, but that was all.
Re. Gail: she said she'd heard from "a lot of people" who basically were "in favor of tolerance" but who felt this was "the wrong time and the wrong kind of statement" [!]. I asked her to tell me when the right time was/is and that, by all means, when that time comes, I hoped all those "people" would speak up and make the right kind of statement.
I'm thinking of recording Lennon's / the Beatles' own versions of "Imagine" & "Let It Be" and printing up the lyrics as handouts and

playing the songs over the PA, if those two boys don't make it back from baseball in time. What do you think?

Doug is going to say something, too, so we have four or five speakers so far.

Karin

Participant #3: The Unitarian Universalist Fellowship

Encouraged by Angela, Rev. Owen, a Unitarian Universalist minister from Suffolk County, asks to participate. I am delighted. I feel tremendous anxiety about the number of participants and fear that no one will show up at the rally. A teacher from our local high school asks about the rally. I solicit her help to reach out to students. My email to a student advisor at the high school doesn't go anywhere.

Date: Wed, 26 Sep 2007, 13:00
Subject: 9/29 rally

122 To Karin, CC: Kim, Angela from Rev. Owen

Karen,

Angela advised me of the rally in Sea Cliff, planned for this Sat. Sept. 25 at 5:00. She asked me to participate as the Minister of the Unitarian Universalist Fellowship. Attached are possible remarks and a prayer. Please let me know if this would be useful in the rally. I would be happy to lend my support to this public expression of solidarity with the lesbian victims of the hate crimes committed, and to the greater Sea Cliff community.

Rev. Owen, UU Fellowship (stranger)

Date: Wed, 26 Sep 2007, 13:39
Subject: 9/29 rally

123 To Rev. Owen from Karin

Dear Rev. Owen,

Thank you so much for your email and suggested remarks. We would love to have you participate on Saturday. Our purpose is not to protest specific crimes and actions, but to repudiate intolerance in general, while affirming solidarity with individuals and groups of every background and persuasion. We want to make this a very positive community event.

In that spirit, I would ask that you delete the stronger, specific references in your statement, such as:

- "to Protest Hate Crimes against Lesbians in Sea Cliff"
- "When the response is jeering, spitting, and epithets, we are horrified."
- "We know that you grieve with us, as we grieve the despicable crimes that have been committed here in Sea Cliff. Our hearts break that we

still suffer such insult and physical abuse."
- "We pray for healing for those who suffered the attacks."

I've scrolled in our press release below, which states the motivation for, and purpose of, our rally. Thanks, again, for your interest in participating. I look forward to welcoming you to Sea Cliff.
Karin

Date: Wed, 26 Sep 2007, 13:01
Subject: SC rally

124 To Audrey, North Shore HS, from Karin
Hi, Audrey.
Is there any interest on the part of students to participate on Saturday? Making music, reading poems? We would love to have young people represented. I'm attaching a simplified flier.
Thanks,
Karin

Date: Wed, 26 Sep 2007, 13:58
Subject: SC rally

125 To Karin from Audrey
hi Karin, have forwarded your question to the gay alliance advisor who was interested in the situation. Hope you hear from her.
Best, Audrey (acquaintance)

Date: Wed, 26 Sep 2007, 14:04
Subject: SC rally

126 To Audrey from Karin
Thanks. I hope to hear from her, too.
Karin

Date: Wed, 26 Sep 2007, 13:05
Subject: SC rally

127 To Sally, North Shore HS student advisor
Hi Sally,
Below is a press release about a "tolerance rally" in Sea Cliff. I don't know if you're aware of it. I'm also attaching a simple flier. Do you think there might be interest on the part of students in participating on Saturday--making a statement, performing music, reading poems? We would love to have young people represented.
Thanks,
Karin

128 To Karin from Sally

I will ask around to see

Response to opposition

I despair of ever getting our purpose across to those who question whether this is the "right time" and the "right place" for a tolerance rally—my friends and neighbors among them. Some people say our purpose is to protest the bar; others that it is "pro-gay." I make another attempt to clarify our purpose, as articulated in our press release and emails: namely that we want to repudiate the damaging headlines by showing that our community embraces tolerance.

Sally **Date: Wed, 26 Sep 2007, 14:57**
Subject: appeal for support

129 To Adam from Karin

I would like to send this out today. Would you like to sign it with me?
Let me know what you think asap.
Karin

"FYI, there is opposition to the Sea Cliff tolerance rally—we still haven't figured out why. We are trying to do something positive and meaningful. One individual is urging village residents not to participate, because: "Sea Cliff does not need this kind of publicity ! whether you are ANTI gay or Pro gay... it does not matter. the final result is that Sea Cliff as a community does not need this kind of exposure . . . Lets stay neutral!!"
Someone else said that a number of people, who are otherwise supportive of tolerance, feel this is the wrong time and the wrong kind of statement. We have not made a statement yet. When is the right time? What is the right kind of statement?
How can we, the Sea Cliff community, remain silent in the face of widespread newspaper and television newscasts and Internet postings, all reporting a "bias-motivated assault," an "anti-gay attack," a "hate crime," a "gay-bashing" in Sea Cliff?
At the very least, let us repudiate intolerance—which is all we are trying to do. Too often we remain silent. Too often we feel it is the wrong time. Too often we feel embarrassed or not certain enough to speak up. This is the perfect time to speak up.
We need your support."

130 To Karin from Adam

It looks good. The only thing I would say is you might want to put a few, He says, " . . ." To make it doubly clear that someone else is saying the things you are putting in quotes. People will skim the email. I would add something simple at the end to crystallize what the message of the rally is. Maybe say something brief that says:

"The purpose of our "rally" is this: to have Sea Cliff residents stand up and demonstrate that they are in favor of tolerance. Nothing more, nothing less. If that is problematic than so be it. Please join us."

That's my two cents. I will gladly add my name to what is below or whatever you add. We are on the same page.

Adam

131 To Adam from Karin

Good advice. Thanks. As soon as I return home from baby-sitting, I'll send it off.

Karin

132 To 45 email contacts from Adam & Karin

FYI, there is opposition to the Sea Cliff tolerance rally—we still have not figured out why. We are trying to do something positive and meaningful. One individual is urging village residents not to participate. He says, "Sea Cliff does not need this kind of publicity ! whether you are ANTI gay or Pro gay... it does not matter. the final result is that Sea Cliff as a community does not need this kind of exposure . . . Lets stay neutral!!"
Someone else said that a number of people, who are otherwise supportive of tolerance, feel this is the "wrong time and the wrong kind of statement" . . . even before we have made a statement. When is the right time? What is the right kind of statement?
How can we, the Sea Cliff community, remain silent in the face of widespread newspaper and television newscasts and Internet postings, all reporting a "bias-motivated assault," an "anti-gay attack," a "hate crime," a "gay-bashing" in Sea Cliff?
At the very least, let us repudiate intolerance—that is our only purpose. Too often we remain silent. Too often we feel it is the wrong time. Too often we feel embarrassed or not certain enough to speak up. This is the

perfect time to speak up.
We need your support. Please join us.
Karin
Adam

Date: Wed, 26 Sep 2007, 21:13
Subject: flier

133 To Karin from Lily

Hi Karin!
I heard thru the grapevine that someone (????) sent you an e-mail about
why the rally is a bad idea. ...If you don't mind, can you forward that to
me, even if it is a piece of shit, I'd like to see what you are up against!
I am really not happy that we'll be gone this weekend. I am distributing
your beautiful flyer as much as I can.
Keep up the great work!
Lily

Date: Wed, 26 Sep 2007, 21:27
Subject: flier

134 To Lily from Karin

Hi Lily,
I just sent you a group email in which the "bad idea" is paraphrased
and/or excerpted. Thanks for your support.
Karin

Date: Wed, 26 Sep 2007, 21:13
Subject: Rally update

135 To Karin from Grace

Karin,
I agree. This is the right time. "If not now, when?" I will be there.
Grace

Date: Wed, 26 Sep 2007, 21:24
Subject: Rally update

136 To Grace from Karin

Thanks, Grace. Your support means a lot.
Karin

Date: Wed, 26 Sep 2007, 21:24
Subject: Rally update

137 To Karin from Adam

You're the goods and should be proud. Peace and Pay it Forward,
Adam

138 To Adam from Karin

Ditto.
Karin

139 To Karin from Kate

karin, i am so sorry to tell you that because my husband's department at nyu is hosting a long-planned anniversary celebration on saturday evening, we won't be able to attend the rally. i feel especially bad about it after receiving this note. i hope the rally is well-attended anyway. we thank you for organizing it and trying to redeem sea cliff's good name.
Kate

140 To Kate from Karin

Kate,
I have been and am so grateful for your email support--right from the start. It means a lot. Thanks,
Karin

141 To Karin from Fred

Dear Karin,
My partner and I are planning on attending the rally this Saturday in Sea Cliff. We have one problem. We're not sure where the park is. I tried putting Sea Cliff Memorial Park in MAPQUEST, but that doesn't seem to be working. Is it possible that you can send directions? We are coming from South Shore, Nassau (Bellmore). Thanks, Karin. We'll see you Saturday!
Sincerely,
Fred

142 To Fred from Karin

Thanks, Fred, for your support. Memorial Park is at the western end of Sea Cliff Avenue, overlooking Hempstead Harbor--an inspiring venue for a hopefully inspiring event. See you Saturday,
Karin

Participant #4: L.I. Community Fellowship

Thanks to Angela's tireless efforts from faraway Puerto Rico, where she is attending a professional conference, the rally gains strength with each additional participant. Angela's support is a wise, benevolent presence that sustains me and keeps me focused.

Date: Thu, 27 Sep 2007, 06:25
Subject: SC Rally

143 To Karin from the Rev. Dr. G. Shane Hibbs, L.I. Community Fellowship

Karin,

Greetings! I was invited by Angela to participate in the rally on Saturday. I was told to send you a transcript of my remarks so it may be reviewed (as you are the organizer). May I ask what type of window of time that remarks are trying to be held to?

I can have remarks to you by tonite. Who will MC this event?

Thanks for the info.

Grace and Peace,

The Rev. Dr. G. Shane Hibbs

Date: Thu, 27 Sep 2007, 10:30
Subject: Rally participants' guidelines

144 To the Rev. Dr. G. Shane Hibbs from Karin

Thank you, Dr. Hibbs, for your support. I think it would be reasonable to not exceed 5-10 minutes--preferably keep it closer to 5. We have all stored up so much to say on this topic and it will be hard to limit ourselves, but I know of no better principle than "less is more" when it comes to public speaking.

You'll find participants' guidelines below. I do insist on reviewing the contributions to ensure that this will be a positive, thoughtful event.

Thanks again, and I look forward to seeing you on Saturday.

Karin

Participants' guidelines

Our purpose is:

to repudiate intolerance in general, affirm our commitment to diversity, and reaffirm our solidarity with people of all backgrounds and persuasions. We want to make this a very positive statement and event that will enhance understanding, empathy and humanity.

Our purpose is not:
to protest specific crimes and actions, nor to discuss what transpired or make judgments or choose sides. There is a criminal investigation underway. In the meantime, however, we cannot ignore widespread newspaper and television coverage, and countless Internet postings that headlined this incident as a "bias-motivated assault," an "anti-gay attack," a "hate crime," a "gay-bashing" in Sea Cliff. We cannot remain silent.

Encouragement
Every encouraging word counts. These supportive emails do wonders.

Date: Thu, 27 Sep 2007, 07:03
Subject: Rally update

145 To Karin from Sophia
Karin...Please do not be disheartened by what a few people think or feel. This feels right to the majority of Sea Cliff I'm sure! I don't think whether you are pro gay is the big picture...I think it has more to do with tolerance of all peoples different from ourselves...some people like to keep their prejudices in the closet and this may be a knocking on the closet door.................Thank you for doing this for us.
Sophia (friend)

Date: Thu, 27 Sep 2007, 10:40
Subject: Rally update

146 To Sophia from Karin
Thanks, Sophia. Your words of wisdom, as always, are a balm on my soul. I love your knocking-on the-closet-door-metaphor & I think you are right on. We are going to make this such a positive, thoughtful event.
Karin

Date: Thu, 27 Sep 2007, 07:13
Subject: Rally update

147 To Karin from Mandy
You are absolutely right Karin - I will try to be there.
Mandy

Date: Thu, 27 Sep 2007, 10:31
Subject: Rally update

148 To Mandy from Karin
Thanks, Mandy. Your support means a lot.
Karin

149 To Karin from Brigitte (friend, former SC resident, living in Switzerland)

Hi Karin,

I just wanted to tell you that I think it's great what you are doing regarding the rally. I heard about what happened from [friends] who just sent me your mail asking people to join. Good luck with it and I'll cross my fingers that lots of residents will participate.

Please say hello to your family for me! When are you coming to Switzerland for a visit again? Take care.

Love,

Brigitte

150 To Brigitte from Karin

Hey Brigitte,

Thanks for your encouragement. It's a no-brainer. We plan a very positive, thoughtful event and yet there are people in Sea Cliff sending me hostile & threatening email. This is not the SC I know and love.

I'll keep you posted.

Tell me how you are and what you are doing.

Love,

Karin

151 To Susan from Karin, response to phone call

It's so good to talk with you, Susan. I'm including here all the things you might have missed:

1. Our most recent email.
2. Participants' guidelines.

Your support means a lot.

Thanks,

Karin

152 To Karin from Susan

Date: Thu, 27 Sep 2007, 11:23
Subject: SC rally

Thank you for sending all the info. It sounds good and very positive. Do you care if I forward to some people or would you prefer to know where it goes?
Susan

153 To Susan from Karin

Date: Thu, 27 Sep 2007, 11:35
Subject: SC rally

Please, please forward it to as many people as you want & have them forward it, as well. I do not have to know where it goes.
Karin

Participant #5: L.I. Gay and Lesbian Youth (LIGALY)

Two days to go. I email Angela for help with encouraging more speakers. She telephones to reassure me. She also heightens my awareness of and sensitivity to language re. the lesbian and gay community. I reword my policy statement to read: "cultures and orientations" rather than "backgrounds and persuasions." I have not heard back from Rev. Owen so I contact him. David Kilmnick from the L.I. Gay and Lesbian Youth asks to participate.

154 To Angela, Mary, Sarah from Karin

Date: Thu, 27 Sep 2007, 11:33
Subject: participants

I have heard from a few individuals who want to speak at the Sea Cliff rally, but not from as many as I was expecting/hoping, based on your emails. You'll find our invitation to participants & guidelines below. I do insist on reviewing the contributions to ensure that this will be a positive, thoughtful event. I've extended the deadline for submitting statements, etc. to Friday, Sept. 28.
Thanks for your support. It means a lot.
Karin

155 To Grace, CC: 45 Karin's contacts from Joan

Date: Thu, 27 Sep 2007, 11:31
Subject: Rally update

This has not changed our minds about attending.
Joan

156 To Karin from Constance

Hello Karin. There are no changes in our plans either. We continue to plan to be there and we are grateful for the opportunity to work positively.
Constance and friends from our church

157 To Rev. Owen from Karin

Dear Rev. Owen,
I thought you would appreciate knowing that you have until Friday, Sept. 28 to submit your contribution. Also, your email yesterday inspired me to clarify guidelines for Sea Cliff rally participants, below. I look forward to seeing you on Saturday.
Karin

158 To Karin from Rev. Owen

With a better understanding of the purpose - thank you - I've edited my earlier version. Let me know what you think.
Rev. Owen

159 To David, LIGALY, from Karin, response to phone call

Hi David,
Thanks for your support. We welcome participation in the form of short pertinent statements, poems, songs, etc. which should be submitted in writing by Friday, Sept. 28. You'll find participants' guidelines below. I do insist on reviewing the contributions to ensure that this will be the positive, thoughtful event.
Thanks again, and I look forward to seeing you on Saturday.
Karin

160 To Karin from Kate

i wish we could be there. we'll be thinking of you.
Kate

U.S. Senate passes hate crimes bill

In a fortuitous coincidence, the Hate Crimes Bill passes in the Senate two days before our tolerance rally. Sarah emails me the Human Rights Campaign press release.

Date: Thu, 27 Sep 2007, 13:53
Subject: FW: PRESS RELEASE:
Senate Passage of Hate Crimes Bill Moves Bill Closer Than Ever To Becoming Law

161 To Karin from Sarah

Karin, the Senate took an historic step today in passing the Hate Crimes bill that has been pending before Congress since Matthew Shepard was murdered over 8 years ago. This is important information to share with those who attend the rally, and it ties in perfectly with our bias incident in Sea Cliff. As I mentioned, I am a member of HRC's board of governors which is why I received this press release.

Sarah

Senate Passage of Hate Crimes Bill Moves Bill Closer Than Ever To Becoming Law
Bill Signifies Major Victory toward Equality for GLBT Community

Senate voted to pass the *Matthew Shepard Act,* which updates and expands the federal hate crimes laws to include bias motivated violence based on a victim's sexual orientation, gender identity, gender, and disability, and provides new resources and tools to assist local law enforcement in prosecuting vicious crimes.

"For over a decade our community has worked tirelessly to ensure protections to combat violence motivated by hate and today we are the closest we have ever been to seeing that become a reality," said Human Rights Campaign President Joe Solmonese. "Congress has taken an historic step forward and moved our country closer to the realization that all Americans, including the GLBT community, are part of the fabric of our nation. The new leadership in Congress fully understands that for too long our community has been terrorized by hate violence. And today, the US Senate has sent a clear message to every corner of our country that we will no longer turn a blind eye to anti-gay violence in America ."

The Senate in a bipartisan vote of 60 to 39 accepted cloture which ended debate on the bill and then moved to approve the *Matthew Shepard Act* by a voice vote -- attaching it as an amendment to the Fiscal Year 2008 Department of Defense Authorization bill.

On May 3rd, the House of Representatives passed a companion bill, the Local Law Enforcement Hate Crimes Prevention Act (H.R. 1592), with a strong bipartisan margin of 237 to 180. Twenty-six state Attorneys General, including

23 from states with anti-hate crimes laws already on the books, as well as 230 law enforcement, civil rights, civic and religious organizations support the Matthew Shepard Act and the LLEHCPA because, despite progress toward equality in almost all segments of our society, hate crimes continue to spread fear and violence and local law enforcement often lack the tools and resources to prevent and prosecute them. Some of these supporting organizations include the National Sheriffs Association, the International Association of Chiefs of Police, 26 state attorneys general, the National District Attorneys Association, the NAACP, the Episcopal Church, the League of Women Voters, the Anti-Defamation League, the Leadership Conference on Civil Rights, the YWCA of the USA and the United Methodist Church .

The President has threatened to veto the legislation, calling it "unnecessary." According to the FBI, 25 Americans each day are victims of hate crimes—that means approximately one hate crime is committed every hour. One in six hate crimes are motivated by the victim's sexual orientation. It's time to update the law to protect everyone, and this year marks our best chance yet to get it done. "Hate crimes terrorize entire communities and violate America's core democratic principles that all citizens are created equal and are afforded equal protection under the law," continued Solmonese. "On behalf of the millions of Americans who have waited too long for these critical protections, we urge President Bush to sign the bill when it arrives on his desk."

The hate crimes amendment was introduced by Sen. Ted Kennedy (D-MA) and Sen. Gordon Smith (R-OR). It confers authority on the federal government to investigate and prosecute crimes committed against victims solely because of their real or perceived sexual orientation, gender, gender identity, and disability when local officials are unwilling or unable to do so. It also expands existing federal hate crimes law to improve prosecution of bias-motivated crimes based on race, religious, national origin and color and provides additional resources to local law enforcement.

The Human Rights Campaign is America's largest civil rights organization working to achieve gay, lesbian, bisexual and transgender equality. By inspiring and engaging all Americans, HRC strives to end discrimination against GLBT citizens and realize a nation that achieves fundamental fairness and equality for all.

Date: Thu, 27 Sep 2007, 17:20
Subject: FW: PRESS RELEASE: Senate Passage of Hate Crimes Bill

162 To Sarah from Karin

Thanks, Sarah,

Good news. Let's hope it passes in the House. You said in your initial email that you would "most likely submit a paragraph on behalf of the Human Rights Campaign." Do you still plan to speak? I hope so. The deadline for submitting contributions is tomorrow. I wanted to be sure you knew that. See you Saturday.

Karin

Hate mail

An imposter claiming to be a "village official" sends Doug a nasty email intended for me. S/He attaches a flier depicting flames—her/his version of a cross-burning, I guess. Confused and appalled, Doug confronts the official via email and I call Village Hall. We learn that an imposter sent the email. Unfortunately, s/he used the organization's email list. Both the village official and I send disclaimers to all recipients of the hate mail. We both contact the Nassau County Police Department.

Date: Thu, 27 Sep 2007, 14:09
Subject: sea cliff protest

163 To Doug and Karin's contacts from "village official"

Karin

This community tolerates you; isn't that enough? You have a lot of nerve claiming to represent the community. You represent your own twisted political interests. Get a life. [Village official]

Message to Karin Barnaby:

164 To [Village official] from Doug

I received an e-mail from you in response to Karin's email to specific members of the community. Was this really sent by you?
Doug

165 To Adam from Karin

This was sent to Doug, but not to me. The second half of addressees is my original list of recipients of yesterday's rally update. The top half is the [community organization's] list. Doug emailed [village official] to ask him if he is the author of this email. We'll see.
Karin

Damage control

The hate mail sender used Natalie's organization's contact list. Under the circumstances, even though I had promised never to use that list again, I feel obliged to send a disclaimer to all hate mail recipients, including the contacts on that list. To post his disclaimer, the Village official uses the organization's email list, as well. This is sure to bring on another public denunciation.

166 To [Village official's] email list from Kate

Dear [Village official],
What an unnecessarily hostile note. Discussion and debate are ennobling. Nasty attacks are just nasty.
Sincerely,
Kate

167 To [village official] impersonator's email list from Karin

PLEASE BE AWARE THAT [Village official] DID NOT SEND THIS MISGUIDED AND HATEFUL EMAIL. SOMEONE IMPERSONATING HIM DID. HOW SAD.
KARIN

168 To Adam from Karin

Date: Thu, 27 Sep 2007, 16:26
Subject: sea cliff protest

Adam, [Village official] did not send this email. We've notified him. Did you open the attachment? We are calling the police.
Karin

Date: Thu, 27 Sep 2007, 16:43
Subject: sea cliff protest

169 To Doug, CC: impersonator's email list from [village official]

The 3:21, 9/27 e-mail signed [Village Official] and sent to Karin was not sent by me. It is obviously from a gutless, cowardly worm with no backbone or integrity. I have been in touch with the police and they are investigating this fraud.
[Village official]

Date: Fri, 28 Sep 2007, 14:13
Subject: sea cliff protest

170 To Doug from Molly

Doug:
So glad - I was worried that dealing with all the Sea Cliff's crazies had finally pushed [village official] over the edge! My money was on Karin in the fight!
Love to Karin!
Molly

Date: Thu, 27 Sep 2007, 17:36
Subject: 9/29 rally

171 To Rev. Owen from Karin

Dear Rev. Owen,
It's a wonderful contribution. I would ask that you not include the title: "Statement at Rally to Protest Hate Crimes Against Lesbians in Sea Cliff." As mentioned, a criminal investigation is underway. For what it's worth, this is not a protest, but a rally. Also, you might want to bring a copy of your statement, in case there are representatives of the press present. See you Saturday.
Thanks.
Karin

172 To Karin from Rev. Owen

Happy to change the title, and I will bring copies. I look forward to meeting you in person, and to participating in this important community event.

Rev. Owen

173 To Joann from Karin

Hi Joann,

I just now thought you might be interested in the "tolerance rally" --for want of a better name—that I've organized for this Saturday, Sept. 29 in Sea Cliff. I was thinking, specifically, of your church and pastor, and their excellent history of advocacy for minorities. Below, I've listed:

1. initial press release

2. most recent email

3. participants' guidelines.

Please know that you, personally, should feel no pressure whatsoever to attend, contribute, or whatever. I just wanted to be sure your pastor was aware, in case he missed the information in the local papers. Sorry for not thinking of this sooner.

Peace,

Karin

174 To Karin from Joann

Hi Karin,

You had actually included me in the first email and I forwarded it along to my pastor. He seemed very interested and I will remind him now that you have reminded me! :) I will forward this email as well so he is fully informed on the guidelines and press release. Thanks for the update.

Joann

175 To Mary from Karin

Hi, Mary.

I'm not sure whether or not you plan to read your poem and/or in some other way participate in Saturday's rally. I hope so. Would you let me know?

Thanks.

Karin

Date: Thu, 27 Sep 2007, 19:34
Subject: Duke reference, flaming poster
176 To Karin from Eloise

Karin,

You have my complete support for the tolerance rally on Saturday; I am becoming very sorry I can't attend the rally but I would put my name on a petition supporting it if one was circulated. I didn't think it takes any courage to support tolerance, but after seeing that hateful message and poster sent to you under the false guise of "Village official," I'm not so sure. Maybe it is good to know someone who thinks that way lives in Sea Cliff; how many others are there? I hope all goes positively on Saturday,

Eloise

Date: Thu, 27 Sep 2007, 20:12
Subject: Duke reference, flaming poster
177 To Eloise from Karin

Thanks. Sad, isn't it?

Karin

Participants #6 & #7: Music!

Date: Thu, 27 Sep 2007, 22:24
An acquaintance puts me in touch with two musicians: a singer, Lorraine, and guitarist, Will, who would love to perform at the rally. I am enormously grateful.

Date: Fri, 28 Sep 2007, 20:44
Subject: Music
178 To Lorraine and Will from Karin

THANKS for lending your talents to the SC Tolerance Rally. Also, Lorraine, thanks for the lyrics of Lennon's "Imagine" & Beatles "Let It Be." That's a huge help. See you tomorrow.

Karin

A great program

Things have shaped up nicely. More confident, I waste little time getting the word out about what I think will be a great event. And then Adam astounds me by proposing to sing a song he's written. It's like icing on the cake.

Date: Fri, 28 Sep 2007, 20:56
Subject: Rally program & purpose

179 To 50 contacts from Karin

At tomorrow's Sea Cliff community rally, eleven individuals will speak/perform, not necessarily in this order:

Karin & Doug, organizers
The Rev. Dr. G. Shane Hibbs, Long Island Community Fellowship
Lorraine, singer; Will, guitarist
Spokesperson, Sea Cliff Methodist Church
David Kilmnick, L.I. Gay and Lesbian Youth
Adam, organizer, singer/songwriter
Rev. Owen, Unitarian Universalist Fellowship
Mary, National Organization for Women

Our purpose is:
to repudiate intolerance, affirm our commitment to diversity, and reaffirm our solidarity with people of all cultures and orientations. We want to make this a very positive statement and event that will enhance understanding and community.

Our purpose is not:
to discuss what transpired or make judgments or protest specific actions that occurred. There is a criminal investigation underway. In the meantime, however, we cannot remain silent.

We have promised all involved and the people of Sea Cliff that we are determined to make this an entirely positive and unifying event. Thanks to all of you, I think we have something really fine in the works.
Karin & Adam

Date: Fri, 28 Sep 2007, 00:00
Subject: sea cliff protest

180 To Karin from Lucy, CC: Doug

Karin-
I just want to say how sorry I am that you are enduring all this rhubarb. You are doing a wonderfully positive thing for everyone in our town. But how typical that when one puts oneself out there, the cowards are so quick to judge. Best of everything with the rally. If we can not be there, we will be there in spirit.
Lucy

181 To Karin from Adam

I was toying with the idea of doing something musical at the event instead of speaking. I had written a song called "We The People" which was basically an anti-administration song. I changed the verses and one line of the chorus.

What do you think, would it be too cheesy to sing a song. I think it may be a bit much, but I'm not sure.

Anyway, attached are the new lyrics and you can listen to the old version of the song by going to www.myspace.com

Let me know what you think.

Adam

182 To Adam from Karin

I LOVE the idea of you singing. You're a man of many gifts, I see/hear. Bravo! I would love to see the lyrics. You should do both--sing AND read your contribution. Why choose one or the other?

See you tomorrow at 10 in the park.

Karin

183 From Adam to Karin

I thought I attached the new lyrics.

184 To Adam from Karin

I'm such a doofus. There was so much to email today that I totally overlooked your attachment. Instead, I went to your site and tried to get the lyrics there.

Your song is totally awesome and I'll never forgive you if you don't sing it. But, read your remarks also. They're so good.

Maybe you should talk to Lorraine, who wants to sing and Will, a student at the HS, who will play the guitar. Polly made the contacts. I've left phone messages with Lorraine and Will, but have not heard back from them.

Re tomorrow: We will be nine individuals speaking/performing (NC Legislator is still unconfirmed): you, Doug & I, one spokesperson for the SC Methodist Church, the Rev. Dr. G. Shane Hibbs of the Long

Island Community Fellowship, Rev. Owen of the Unitarian Universalist Fellowship, and David Kilmnick of L.I. Gay and Lesbian Youth. Lorraine & and North Shore HS student, Will, will play guitar and sing. All are asked to speak between 5 to 10 minutes, preferably shorter than longer. Less is more. I informed everyone that we've promised all involved and the people of Sea Cliff that we are determined to make this an entirely positive and unifying event. As mentioned in the guidelines below, our purpose is not to protest specific crimes and actions, nor to discuss what transpired or make judgments. Hence any mention of specifics should be avoided. We do not want to give those who are opposed to this event—and there are some—any justification for their opposition/hostility. We insist that these guidelines be followed. Did you ever hear from the three *Newsday* reporters? Brenda, a writer & former SC resident with connections to *Newsday* & *News 12* phoned & asked if she should contact them. I said yes & gave her all the pertinent info. I think we have something really fine in the works.
Karin

Date: Fri, 28 Sep 2007, 07:23
Subject: village official imposter

185 To Karin from Gail

Dearest Karin,
I just read the "village official" emails. I can't believe what you're having to deal with here just because you're trying to do something good. I'm so sorry - I hope they catch the "gutless worm."
XO,
Gail

Date: Fri, 28 Sep 2007, 08:18
Subject: Rally

186 To Karin from Brigitte

Hi Karin,
Jeeze, that is unbelievable. You know, the whole world is not the one we used to know. Random violence is thriving here in Zurich. It's gotten so bad that the right wingers want to instill draconian type laws against "Ausländer [foreigners]." It's a mess actually. Unfortunately though it usually is somebody from the Balkans that ends up comitting these crimes, (stabbings, rape, assault, etc...). I think the world is going to hell in a handbasket.
Why on earth would you get hate mail? Who is it coming from? Do they have the guts to actually sign their name?
I'm sorry that this is happening. You of all people certainly don't deserve

hostile and threatening mail.

Take care and stay safe!! There are lots of weirdos on this planet for sure!!

L, Brigitte

PS Did you ever publish your novel? I'd love to read it. :-)
PPS We are all doing well chugging along. Work is a bit dull, but what can you do? ;-)

Date: Fri, 28 Sep 2007, 04:46
Subject: Rally participants' guidelines

187 To Karin from the Rev. Dr. G. Shane Hibbs

Karin,

Please find a draft of my speech for saturday pasted below. I can try to give you a final draft today; however, there will be minor changes to this. Please let me know if this fits within your qualifications. My goal was to make it so. I look forward to hearing from you.

Grace and Peace,

The Rev. Dr. G. Shane Hibbs

Date: Fri, 28 Sep 2007, 11:21
Subject: Rally participants' guidelines

188 To the Rev. Dr. G. Shane Hibbs from Karin

Dear Rev. Francis,

Your speech will be a wonderful contribution.

I would call your attention to two references that I would ask you to delete and replace with milder language. I have promised all involved and the people of Sea Cliff that we are determined to make this an entirely positive and unifying event. As mentioned in the guidelines, our purpose is not to protest specific crimes and actions, nor to discuss what transpired or make judgments or choose sides. Hence any judgment about specifics should be avoided. We do not want give those who are opposed to this event—and there are those—any justification for their opposition/hostility. I've itemized my suggestions below.

Thank you for your support and participation.

Karin

1. First paragraph, third & fourth sentence:
"In this village several months ago, a horrific act of hatred took place. It was an unconscionable act that a group of persons would attack others simply for being different."

* I don't want to put words into your mouth, but just to give you a sense of the tone, I would suggest something along the lines of: "I am pleased to be here today, standing united, shoulder to shoulder with a community that is willing to speak out and take a stand. We have come together as an act of unity . . . with people of all cultures and orientations. Similar or different, we are all equal.

2. Second to last paragraph, second sentence:
"Indifference breeds contempt in the heart of humanity. Therefore we assemble ourselves that we may inscribe in our hearts and stamp indelibly into our memories this horrible act of hatred that we may never provide lethargic apathy, but instead be challenged in every part of our lives to stand as one community."

* It would be good to change "this horrible act of hatred" to read "any act of hatred." Also, I corrected a typo in the first sentence to read "breeds" (I am a proofreader/editor by profession).

Date: Fri, 28 Sep 2007, 09:02
Subject: Rally participants' guidelines

189 To Karin from the Rev. Dr. G. Shane Hibbs
Karin,
Thank you so much. I appreciate your suggestions and will make those changes. It is my pleasure to be speaking and I understand your purpose. So please know that it is my intent to help make this a successful event. May I ask roughly what time you expect me to speak? How long will the event be? Thanks.
Grace and Peace,
The Rev. Dr. G. Shane Hibbs

Date: Fri, 28 Sep 2007, 12:22
Subject: Rally participants' guidelines

190 To the Rev. Dr. G. Shane Hibbs from Karin
Thanks for your understanding. We start at 5. There are 6 speakers and 2-3 singer/musicians. It shouldn't last more than an hour or so. Memorial Park is at the western end of Sea Cliff Avenue, overlooking Hempstead Harbor. You might want to bring a copy of your remarks, in case the press attends. They usually like to have hard copy. Thank you for participating.
See you at 5 tomorrow.
Karin

191 To Karin from Mary

Seems like you're having a bit of trouble rallying the troops. I plan to be there and participate -- will read my 5-line poem with title, with a few introductory remarks.

It should all take about 3 or 4 minutes. Same place? Same time?   Please confirm.

Om

Mary

192 To Mary from Karin

I'm so glad. Yes, same time, same place, Memorial Park, at the west end of Sea Cliff Avenue, overlooking beautiful Hempstead Harbor. I understand the weather gods will be smiling on our rally, as well.

Om to you, too (very nice)

Karin

193 To Karin, Mary, Sarah, CC: 3 contacts from Angela

Karen,

My perception is people want to be present in solidarity, and may not necessarily feel speaking is within their comfort zone. Don't let the low number of respondents who are asking to speak mislead you. What is important is that a community response is happening, that the silence will be broken. This is a message that goes beyond the numbers of attendees. I am so glad to hear that one of the local churches will be there in solidarity. I will forward the invite to speak around one more time :)

Warmly,

Angela

194 To Karin from Lily

Karin, Your flyer is now on the Bulletin board of the Gay and Lesbian Community Center on W. 13th St.

Whoever penned that stupid letter in opposition to your rally is actually stimulating interest in the community and getting people motivated, right?

I'll be thinking of you most fervently tomorrow...

In loving friendship, Lily

Date: Fri, 28 Sep 2007, 11:42
Subject: Sea Cliff Rally

195 To Karin from Jason

Go Karin!

If you're pissing off some hateful bastards you must be doing something right!

I'll be at the rally and I appreciate and applaud your efforts.

Jason

Date: Fri, 28 Sep 2007, 11:52
Subject: our phone conversation

196 To Karin from Dean, follow-up to phone call

Hi Karen--This is such a delicate issue and I do commend you for taking a stand. I'm in agreement with you 100% as far as tolerance is concerned and if I was to witness "any" bias incident I would put myself in harms way to prevent violence. Where we differ is that, unlike yourself, I really feel that the rally will be perceived as a response to what happened at Partners and even an indictment over it. And in regards to that incident my gut tells me that neither side were angels.

I know you said that the rally has nothing to do with what happened at Partners, and though I know that's your gut feeling, I just can't see it that way. It's quite obvious to me that you are following your conscience and doing what you think is right. I only wish I could be in full agreement with you but I'm not.

I wish you the best and hope all goes well.

Dean

Date: Fri, 28 Sep 2007, 14:34
Subject: our phone conversation

197 To Dean from Karin

Thanks, Dean, for your call and email.

I don't know if you've received any of my emails & such, so I am including them below. I think that would be the best way to clarify what the rally is and is not about. It is not, for example, a "pro-gay gathering" as Bob states. The fact that he is characterizing it as such AND getting such a strong response against it should tell us all something about Sea Cliff.

FYI: You say that I said: "the rally has nothing to do with what happened at Partners." I said: "the rally *will* not have anything to do with Partners."

We have promised all involved and the people of Sea Cliff that we are determined to make this an entirely positive and unifying event. As mentioned in the guidelines below, our purpose is not to protest specific actions and crimes, nor to discuss what transpired or make judgments. Hence any mention of specifics will be avoided.

Thanks,

Karin

Participant #8: Nassau County Legislator
Bless our NC Legislator. She is the only elected official to want to participate.

Date: Fri, 28 Sep 2007, 12:33
Subject: Rally in Sea Cliff

198 To Karin from Nassau County Legislator's office

Adam suggested that I contact you regarding the rally this Saturday. [NC Legislator who represents Sea Cliff] plans to attend the rally in order to add her support. If you get this in time and would like her to speak please e-mail me back (otherwise you can just talk to her tomorrow). If you don't want her to speak that is fine as well, she is still going to try to attend. Thanks.

Bruce, Legislative Aide, NC Legislator

Date: Fri, 28 Sep 2007, 12:39
Subject: Rally in Sea Cliff

199 To Bruce [legislative aide] from Karin

Hi Bruce,

We would be delighted to have [NC Legislator} attend and speak. We will be gathering at 5 p.m. at Sea Cliff's Memorial Park which is at the western end of Sea Cliff Avenue, overlooking Hempstead Harbor. The entire rally should last about 1 to 1 1/2 hours.

It would be helpful for [NC Legislator] to know as much background as possible about this event—hence the lengthy email.

We will be eight individuals speaking/performing (incl. NC Legislator): three SC residents, one spokesperson for the SC Methodist Church, the Rev. Dr. G. Shane Hibbs of the Long Island Community Fellowship, Rev. Owen of the Unitarian Universalist Fellowship, and David Kilmnick of L.I. Gay and Lesbian Youth. North Shore HS students will play guitar and sing. All are asked to speak between 5 to 10 minutes, preferably shorter than longer. Less is definitely more at such a gathering.

We have promised all involved and the people of Sea Cliff that we are determined to make this an entirely positive and unifying event. As mentioned in the guidelines below, our purpose is not to protest specific crimes and actions, nor to discuss what transpired or make judgments. Hence any mention of specifics should be avoided. We do not want to give those who are opposed to this event--and there are a few/many--any justification for their opposition/hostility. We insist that these guidelines be followed.

Included below:
1. participants' guidelines.
2. my initial press release
3. my most recent email

We look forward to seeing NC Legislator tomorrow.
Thanks for your support,
Karin Barnaby

Date: Fri, 28 Sep 2007, 12:41
Subject: Sea Cliff rally

200 To Karin from David Kilmnick, L.I. Gay and Lesbian Youth (LIGALY)

Hi Karin -
Thanks for putting together this very important rally. I have put together a 2 minute speech to be read at tomorrow's rally. Look forward to seeing you tomorrow. Take care -
David

Date: Fri, 28 Sep 2007, 13:50
Subject: Sea Cliff rally

201 To David from Karin

Hi David,
We would love for you to speak. We will be gathering at 5 p.m. at Sea Cliff's Memorial Park which is at the western end of Sea Cliff Avenue, overlooking Hempstead Harbor. The entire rally should last about 1 to 1½ hours. We will be eight individuals speaking/performing: three SC residents, one spokesperson for the SC Methodist Church, the Rev. Dr. G. Shane Hibbs of the Long Island Community Fellowship, Rev. Owen of the Unitarian Universalist Fellowship, and you of L.I. Gay and Lesbian Youth. North Shore HS students will play guitar and sing. All are asked to speak between 5 to 10 minutes, preferably shorter than longer. Less is definitely more at such a gathering.

I encourage you to read our participants' guidelines, below. We have promised all involved and the people of Sea Cliff that we are determined to make this an entirely positive and unifying event. As mentioned in the guidelines, our purpose is not to protest specific crimes and actions, nor to discuss what transpired or make judgments. Hence any mention of specifics should be avoided. We do not want to give those who are opposed to this event--and there are a few/many--any justification for their opposition/hostility. We insist that these guidelines be followed. With that in mind, I think your first paragraph is great, but would ask that you delete and/or replace most of your second paragraph. Please submit your final remarks to me before tomorrow. Thanks for your understanding.

Karin

Date: Fri, 28 Sep 2007, 17:24
Subject: Sea Cliff rally

202 To Karin from David, LIGALY

Hi Karin -

Thanks for getting back to me so quickly. I think we put together a very very short speech that fits within the guidelines. To avoid mentioning what had happened would ignore what has galvanized all to come out -- simply that it took an incident like this to bring us together. It also would keep the incident "in the closet" so to speak, which our community would not feel very good about (we have surveyed more than a dozen Sea Cliff residents re: this). However, now that we're all together lets move forward in a show of unity and make sure we don't let these incidents happen again anywhere. Look forward to hearing from you again and thanks once again for taking the leadership to bring everyone together!

David

Date: Fri, 28 Sep 2007, 18:23
Subject: Sea Cliff rally

203 To David from Karin

David,

I am keenly aware of what galvanized this response since I am very much a part of it. I will speak first and will mention it in terms of the widespread headlines--which I will quote verbatim-- that appeared in newspapers, on TV and Internet sites worldwide.

Trust me on this one. As enlightened as most of Sea Cliff is, there is a virulent minority--here, as anywhere else--that is hostile & spreading misinformation. We do not want to give them the least iota of ammunition. I would like to see your final draft. Also, bring hard copies along in case the press is in attendance.

Thanks,

Karin

204 To Karin from Millie (former Sea Cliff resident)

Dear Karin,
Constance was kind enough to forward your E-mail to me. I just wanted
to express my support and wish you well. I would be there if I could.
Here is a poem you might like to use -an old Irish prayer:

Deep peace of the running waves to you.
Deep peace of the floating air to you.
Deep peace of the smiling stars to you.
Deep peace of the quiet earth to you.
Deep peace of the watching shepherds to you.
Deep peace of the Son of Peace to you...

I'll be thinking of you,
Millie

205 To Millie from Karin

Thanks, Millie
It means a lot to have your good thoughts & support coming at me from
wherever you are.
Peace,
Karin

206 To Karin from Brenda

Hi Karin, I got this email from a friend (are you the Karin from
Roots?) I'm going to try to make it...wondered if you had contacted
News 12 to come? I can call if you'd like (I do media work). But fyi, the
assignment desk is Assignment Desk (breaking or regular news
coverage): 516-393-1390 / select 1 or 2. Also, did you let the folks at
Newsday know? This would be a great story. If you need any help, please
feel free to call me. I used to live on Prospect, I think we may have been
neighbors many years ago?
Brenda

207 To Brenda from Karin, follow-up to phone call

Hi Brenda.

Great talking with you. Below is all the pertinent info. Thanks in advance for anything you can do.

Karin

We will be gathering at 5 p.m. at Sea Cliff's Memorial Park which is at the western end overlooking Hempstead Harbor. The entire rally should last about 1 to 1 ½ hours.

We will be nine individuals speaking/performing (incl. NC Legislator): three SC residents, one spokesperson for the SC Methodist Church, the Rev. Dr. G. Shane Hibbs of the Long Island Community Fellowship, Rev. Owen of the Unitarian Universalist Fellowship, and David Kilmnick of L.I. Gay and Lesbian Youth. North Shore HS students will play guitar and sing. All are asked to speak between 5 to 10 minutes, preferably shorter than longer. Less is definitely more at such a gathering.

We have promised all involved and the people of Sea Cliff that we are determined to make this an entirely positive and unifying event. As mentioned in the guidelines below, our purpose is not to protest specific crimes and actions, nor to discuss what transpired or make judgments. Hence any mention of specifics should be avoided. We do not want to give those who are opposed to this event--and there are a some--any justification for their opposition/hostility. We insist that these guidelines be followed.

208 To Karin from Brenda

Thank you Karin!

209 To Brenda from Karin

Any "in" with the New York Times? I think we owe them a chance to be in on a really big & wonderful story :-)

Karin

210 To Karin from Brenda

Unfortunately, no! I wish I did! They don't do nearly enuf LI coverage.

211 To Brenda from Karin

I know. Even their Sunday "Long Island" section is always all about
New Jersey.
I'll try to find someone to send something to.
Karin

212 To Mary from Karin

I'm about to send a final email re our purpose & program tomorrow.
I wanted to be sure that I mentioned to you that we are not discussing
the Partner's assault or making judgments about or protesting the specific
actions there. As enlightened as most of Sea Cliff is, there seems to be a
virulent minority--here, as anywhere else--that is spreading
misinformation & poison. We do not want to give them the least iota of
ammunition. Thanks for your understanding.
I think we have something really fine in the works.
Karin

More kindness from the Smiths

213 To Karin from the Smiths

Let us know what we can do if you need our help to set up for the rally
tomorrow... I noticed that Bob has e-mailed me and everyone else again
about his total e-mail response . . . I don't think he liked my response to
his first posting . . . let us know if we can help in any way
the Smiths

214 To the Smiths from Karin

Since you ask, I would love to know your first names :-)
I will send a last email in a little while to give everyone a sense of what to

expect. I think we have something really fine in the works.
Your support has been and your attendance will be much appreciated.
Thank you, thank you,
Karin

Date: Fri, 28 Sep 2007, 20:47
Subject: If you need any help?

215 To Karin from the Smiths

Sorry. I should have included that. I'm Chris and my wife is Peggy. We
have 4 young children who will be joining us at the rally as well.
The Smiths

Date: Fri, 28 Sep 2007, 21:00
Subject: If you need any help?

216 To the Smiths from Karin

Bless you.
Karin

Date: Sat, 29 Sep 2007, 09:03
Subject: Niemoeller

217 To the Smiths from Karin

Chris,
Would you like to read your excellent quote of and statement about
Niemoeller at the rally today? It would be a great contribution. Any
remarks would have to eliminate references to any of the specifics of the
incident & we're not mentioning Partners.
Let me know.
Karin

Date: Fri, 28 Sep 2007, 22:11
Subject: Your statement

218 To Sarah from Karin

Hi Sarah,
I've been so busy, I suddenly realized that I have not received your
statement for the Human Rights Campaign. I have asked everyone to
submit their drafts to me and they have. Do you think you could get it to
me tomorrow morning? You are planning to say something, aren't you?
Karin

Date: Fri, 28 Sep 2007, 23:22
Subject: Update

219 To Karin from Adam

Hi Karin, we just got back from a comedy club. My whole head is still
hurting from my laughing so much. We had a blast. I've been really

anxious about all that has transpired. I had kind of decided not to sing the song because I don't really know the new lyrics and I tend to get nervous for performance, but maybe I need to throw a little more caution to the wind.

I loved what you wrote and I really would love if we don't even mention Partners specifically. Natalie sent out a nasty letter saying why she wasn't coming.

Let's leave all of the windbags behind and make this a celebration. The Smiths left a message on my machine asking if there was anything they could do to help.

Can we meet at 9:30 tomorrow instead of 10a.m. It turns out that my son has an early birthday party. No, I never heard back from any of the *Newsday* columnists, nor did I hear anything from *News12*.

As far as the person who's playing guitar, do they have an acoustic/electric or an electric guitar? Do they need a mic for the guitar or are they going to "plug in direct." If they need a mic, I believe I have an extra to mic it if we need to.

Thanks for the kind words about the song!

Peace,

Adam

Peace and Pay it Forward,

Date: Sat, 29 Sep 2007, 08:51
Subject: Update

220 To Adam from Karin

No one is mentioning Partners, not even a bar. Will is playing an acoustic guitar. What did Natalie say? I'm putting out a call for a photographer/filmmaker to document today's rally.

See you at 9:30.

Karin

Date: Sat, 29 Sep 2007, 12:18
Subject: the rally

221 To Karin from Gail

Thought you might like to see this.

Gail

Forwarded Message -----

Sent: Saturday, September 29, 2007 11:16 AM
From: Nancy
Subject: the rally

To Gail from Nancy

Hi, Gail. Since I will be away this afternoon into this evening, I am unable to attend the rally. But I wanted to express my support

for the proposition for which the rally stands. I don't know who Bob is, however, to say he is clueless is an understatement. He just doesn't get it. However, he is not alone. I've heard some comments about what happened on the night of 9/1, and some (certainly not all) disappointed me. I didn't feel there was enough outrage or distaste for the actions of the ten alleged perpetrators from Partners that night. And indeed, even heard people express sentiments that "the women should have known better." --In my mind, that is blaming the alleged victims for the deplorable actions that were leveled at them. Whether this is played out in a court of law or there is a quick plea taken, if this indeed happened, we need to condemn this kind of behavior and reinforce our commitment to tolerance and acceptance. I know that is what the majority of SC residents represent.
Nancy

Date: Sat, 29 Sep 2007, 15:38
Subject: Rally program & purpose

222 To Karin from Elaine

Dear Karin,
This looks excellent. I applaud what you have created.
Sincerely,
Elaine

Date: Sat, 29 Sep 2007, 09:08
Subject: last thoughts

223 To 50 contacts from Karin

Are there any photographers/filmmakers out there who are willing and able to document the Sea Cliff rally? Please call me.
FYI, there are no toilets and there is no seating at the park. Bring your own chairs and/or blankets.
See you later,
Karin

Date: Sat, 29 Sep 2007, 14:11
Subject: Sea Cliff rally 9/29

224 To LIdesk@news12.com from Karin (response to phone call from News12)

At the Sea Cliff community rally, eleven individuals will speak/perform, not necessarily in this order:

Karin & Doug Barnaby, residents
The Rev. Dr. G. Shane Hibbs, L. I. Community Fellowship

Lorraine, singer
Will, guitarist
Spokesperson, Sea Cliff Methodist Church
David Kilmnick, L.I. Gay and Lesbian Youth
Adam, singer/songwriter
Rev. Owen, Unitarian Universalist Fellowship
Mary, National Organization for Women
Nassau County Legislator

We have promised all involved and the people of Sea Cliff that we are determined to make this an entirely positive and unifying event. As mentioned in the guidelines below, our purpose is not to protest specific crimes and actions, nor to discuss what transpired or make judgments.

Included below:
1. initial press release
2. participants' guidelines.
3. most recent email publicity

The Sea Cliff Tolerance Rally
Memorial Park, Sea Cliff
September 29, 2007, 5 p.m.

1. "Imagine," John Lennon, performed by Lorraine & Will
2. Karin, Sea Cliff resident
3. Doug, Sea Cliff resident
4. Rev. Owen, Unitarian Universalist Fellowship
5. Spokesperson, Sea Cliff Methodist Church
6. Mary, National Organization for Women
7. David Kilmnick, L.I. Gay and Lesbian Youth
8. The Rev. Dr. G. Shane Hibbs, L.I. Community Fellowship
9. Nassau County Legislator
10. Adam, Sea Cliff resident, singer/songwriter; "We the People"
11. "Let It Be," the Beatles, performed by Lorraine &Will

Statement - Karin

Something happened here in Sea Cliff between two groups of people, late at night, inside and outside a bar. We are not here to discuss what transpired or make judgments. There is an investigation underway. In the meantime, however, widespread newspaper and television coverage, and countless Internet postings headlined this incident as a "bias-motivated assault," an "anti-gay attack," a "hate crime," a "gay-bashing" in Sea Cliff.

That is why we are here. How can we ignore these headlines? How can we not address these issues? How can we not search our own conscience? How can we remain silent? At the very least, let us repudiate intolerance. Now. Here. Too often we remain silent. Too often we feel it's the wrong time. Too often we feel embarrassed or not certain enough to speak up. Too often we fear that we won't be heard or that we won't make a difference . . . None of these reasons is good enough. We *can* make a difference. Now. Here. In Sea Cliff.

"Think globally, act locally"– I first heard that slogan when I was active in environmental initiatives some years ago. That is what we are doing here today: thinking globally, acting locally. We are acting, now, here, to affirm our community's commitment to diversity and to reaffirm our solidarity with people of all cultures and orientations, races and religions.

For as long as I've known and loved Sea Cliff –I've lived here for 40 years—it has embraced diversity, creativity, and eccentricity. The Sea Cliff I know and love *is* a live-and-let-live community. The Sea Cliff I know and love *is* a safe haven for non-conformists. What matters in the Sea Cliff I know and love is authenticity: to fully be who and what you are and allow everyone else to fully be who and what they are . . . I say these things in the present tense; I would hate to ever have to change them to the past tense.

I'd like to say something about intolerance. Intolerance always goes hand in hand with ignorance. Intolerance and ignorance are the twin evils that have historically caused most the world's violence and suffering and they continue to do so today, with a vengeance. They polarize and tear people apart, pit neighbor against neighbor, nation against nation, religion against religion, ethnic group against ethnic group. It doesn't have to be this way, but it is. And it will continue this way for as long as there are ruthless individuals willing to exploit ignorance and fear to consolidate their power or . . . to get elected. No easier, sure-fire, tried-and-true method to manipulate public opinion exists, than to ridicule or demonize some minority only to subsequently justify its marginalization, disenfranchisement, persecution and ultimately, if left unchecked, its annihilation. These ruthless individuals who seek power by scape-goating and fear-mongering are surely the bane of humanity.

Abroad, these individuals claim to be following God's will in order to give themselves license to maim, torture and mass murder all those who are different or who just happen to get in their way. Here, somewhat more subtly, they claim political and religious principles to justify their greed for power. They disguise their scape-goating and fear-mongering with the thinly-veiled bigotry of pious slogans like "family values," "defending the sanctity of marriage" and, most ludicrous of all: "Christian values," to disenfranchise their fellow citizens and exclude them from enjoying the rights and legal protections that every American is entitled to.

What a far cry *their* "Christian values" are from the original Christian values: from that loving, inclusive message of 2000 years ago, the message of a gentle carpenter named Jesus who assembled a family of his choosing: a woman and a dozen or so men—how's that for an alternative lifestyle?—to spread the message of humility, kindness, charity and love. Acting ever so locally, so long ago, in that distant place, he gave us the miraculous revelation of the human spirit, a place that exists within each one of us, that transcends suffering and violence, poverty and ignorance; where we are all equally created in God's image: male and female, heterosexual and homosexual, white and black and brown, tall and short, handsome and homely, smart and not so; and where we are all equally blessed with grace.

This lowly carpenter changed the world two thousand years ago. We can change the world, now, here, in Sea Cliff.

Statement - Doug

I moved to Sea Cliff with my wife Karin 40 years ago, after discovering it one day while driving to a painting class with local artist, Harold Stevenson. What impressed me so much about the Village was its unpretentiousness and diversity—its friendly, hometown feel. That's why we moved here. Many others have moved here for the same reasons.

What has been troubling me is the negative press Sea Cliff has received over the past few years—especially because I know it does not accurately reflect what Sea Cliff is, and who we are. There have been lawsuits against the Village alleging racial bias and anti-Semitism, and now, within the last month, we have had worldwide headlines about another bias incident in the Village.

Even though the lawsuits were struck down, the publicity has impacted negatively on the reputation of Sea Cliff, as has this latest incident. I do not want Sea Cliff to lose its attractiveness, or to see people and families feel discouraged from living here

In his book, *The Tipping Point*, Malcolm Gladwell describes how a series of seemingly small events can lead to major changes, for good or ill. For example, New York City's past crime epidemic was reversed by the MTA, when it initiated a campaign of addressing the small issues first: fare beating, graffiti, etc. This sent a message that it was not going to be "business as usual." These seemingly small steps eventually led to a major reduction in crime.

Here in Sea Cliff, we need to address what some view as the smaller problems and issues of a typical late night fight between drunks at a bar, because of the previous bias allegations. If we don't, Sea Cliff will eventually suffer the larger consequences. This latest incident brings us that much closer to a "tipping point," whether it will take the form of Sea Cliff losing its reputation for tolerance or its attractiveness or its sense of community.

This is why we're here. We want to send a message. With this rally, we hope not only to maintain our reputation, but maybe even to have a wider impact on the larger issues of intolerance and injustice in the world.

Statement - Rev. Owen, Unitarian Universalist Fellowship

You would think that everyone would celebrate love wherever it is expressed. Just as onlookers enjoy an elderly couple dancing together, clearly enjoying each other's embrace, and just as we enjoy the prospect of fresh love in a young couple's exuberant dance, so you would think we would enjoy the affection that two women, or two men dancing together exude. You would think that the religions of the world that teach that God is fundamentally love would celebrate love in its many forms.

However, we know too well that humans use religion to justify their fears, their ignorance. Fundamentalists of all stripes (Christian, Jewish, Muslim, Hindu, Buddhist) use religion to hate those who differ from themselves. Instead of a God of love, they worship a God of hatred and violence against other humans.

I stand here, with my religious colleagues, to uphold the God of love. This God glories in love in all its expressions. Does love guide us? That's the profound question we must ask again and again. The prophets are many who confront us with this question: Isaiah, Jesus, Mohammed, Rumi, Buddha, Starhawk, Gandhi, Martin Luther King, Jr., and so many more.

As we gather to affirm that love that is glad whenever, and however, love unfolds among us, I invite you to listen as I pray.

God of love, named in many different ways, and, for others, unnamed, in your infinite playfulness, you have created us each unique – one-of-a-kind - yet one in our capacity to love, however we express that love. We know that you grieve with us, whenever intolerance for difference acts out. You suffer with us.

Spirit of love and life, help us all to heal. We pray for healing for those who suffer from acts of prejudice. We pray that their pride and confidence may be restored that they may celebrate their love publicly and unafraid – that they might dance together anywhere and be joyous and un-self-conscious.

We pray for healing for our community. We pray that we may restore our community's pride that we accept and embrace the many different ways that love is savored among us.

We pray for healing for those who injure others. As tempted as we are to hurt them in turn, we know that hatred never overcomes hatred; only love can overcome hatred. We know that prejudice and violence often takes root in a person who has been brutalized him or herself. And so we pray for their souls that they may come to a deeper wisdom, and realize the hurt they have done; that they might seek forgiveness for the injury caused by prejudice and intolerance.

As tempting as it is, feeling the deep anger and rage at hurt suffered, we pray for ourselves that we may find that encompassing compassion that forgives even the most grievous hurt, when people who cause hurt realize what they have done and seek restoration.

Spirit of love and justice, we are grateful for those who have gathered in solidarity to promote the full acceptance of love in its many forms. We commit ourselves again, and again, to the ongoing work of overcoming ignorance and fear, which so often attacks others. Strengthen us in our resolve to create the beloved community in which all love is savored.

We pray in the spirit that we, in our many ways, find holy, Amen.

Mission Statement - Spokesperson, Sea Cliff Methodist Church

The Mission of the United Methodist Church of Sea Cliff is to carry out God's purposes as defined for us by the life of Jesus Christ. As His disciples we seek to reach out to our own community and the world to support God's work and to invite, without exclusion, all people to a life of love and service in Jesus' name. We pray that your time with us will be a joyful celebration of life and faith.

"Open Hearts, Open Minds, Open Doors"

The People of the United Methodist Church

Poem - Mary, National Organization for Women (NOW)

Here is a very short poem I wrote in 1990 - during a hateful period of race bias -- if you are old enough, perhaps you will remember it - a black man named Yusuf Hawkins had the misfortune of walking through the Bensonhurst neighborhood in Brooklyn -- and was chased to his death.

Love Thy Neighbor
or
Tolerance 101

Red headlines tell the tale of Yusuf Hawkins,
victim of the word made manifest.
I fear the hate that flickered like a flame that night,
igniting other coiled pockets of hate
as it flashed its way to death.

Statement – David Kilmnick, L.I. Gay and Lesbian Youth (LIGALY)

In the shuffle of everyday life we find ourselves thrown into categories that separate us from one another; our race, our sex, our sexual orientation, our gender identity. We are reminded of our differences every time we are asked to fill out a form. Although we cannot ignore our differences, sometimes, we need to remember and celebrate our similarities. We as a community must stand together as one force that will not tolerate people being targeted because of their differences. We need to treat this incident as an attack on our community not just an attack on an individual or a group of individuals.

As a representative of the Anti-Violence Project - Long Island at Long Island Gay and Lesbian Youth it is an extreme disappointment to hear of such acts of hate happening right here in our backyard. AVP-LI provides comprehensive services to gay, lesbian, bisexual and transgender (GLBT) survivors of violence as well as conduct trainings to educate about the dynamics of violence faced by GLBT people. The violence that has occurred here and given a reputation to this town is precisely what AVP-LI aims to eliminate from our community. It is unfortunate that it had to take a person with a high profile to be attacked before a problem is identified and recognized by the general public. Now it is our responsibility to ensure that this kind of thing doesn't happen again here or anywhere else on Long Island.

Statement - The Rev. Dr. G. Shane Hibbs, L.I. Community Fellowship

I am pleased to be here today, standing united, shoulder to shoulder with a community that is willing to speak out and take a stand. We have come together as an act of unity . . . with people of all cultures and orientations. Similar or different, we are all equal. Equality is not a negotiable standard; it is a societal tenet. We have come together to be reminded of what is now required of us: to speak of unity, equality, and justice.

In any given situation, we have the opportunity to grow as a community. Through the face of adversity, we have the opportunity to be conquerors, to create change, and to be more than we were yesterday.

We must learn from today that the morality of equality is a necessity of life. We will not negotiate, we will not compromise, and we will not surrender the inalienable right for all persons to be treated with respect equally. We have come to a precipice and stand at the edge of great divide in our country, in our states, and in our local communities. Now we must embrace one another and realize that by the power of the great creator above, we are all God's children.

We have been called by many, a Christian nation. Equality is a Christian principle. Without each and every person standing united in the face of hatred, in the face of prejudices, in the face of discrimination, then we will all be victims of inequality. The inaction of one leads to the great injustice of hatred for all humanity.

You are my brother and you are my sister. Let us walk with one another, hand in hand in the bonds of God's gracious love and let us be united as we stand against these indignant acts. Indifference breeds contempt in the heart of humanity. Therefore we assemble ourselves that we may inscribe in our hearts and stamp indelibly into our memories every act of hatred that we may never provide lethargic apathy, but instead be challenged in every part of our lives to stand as one community.

Let us work towards the day that each and every person can walk down the street holding the hand of the person they love without fear of retribution. Let us hope for the day.
Copyright 2010 G. Shane Hibbs. Printed with permission.

Statement – Nassau County Legislator

We need to teach our young people tolerance. Very often our children's' behavior reflects our own feelings or prejudices. When we teach that those who differ from us are somehow inferior . . . inferior people who pose a threat to us . . . we learn to spread hate and fear throughout our community. Young people learn what they see and hear from each other and from their elders. They learn how to swear and use harsh words to hurt one another.

The more we lead by example that we are all one people...joined together by a common desire to live and prosper in a common cause, the more we show that acceptance of one another is essential to our collective survival. Instilling in young people that we must all share this increasingly smaller world with displays of kindness and consideration will enhance all of our lives.

When you teach a child to hate all of us are degraded. When you teach that someone who is different from you is a threat to you, you make it easier for hate to grow with violence being the end result. By teaching love, patience and understanding you make hate difficult and violence virtually impossible. Dream of a world without hate.

Look around and you will see many differences among us . . . we all come from different races, ethnic groups and religions. We differ on our size, sexual orientation, and our opinions. Our neighbor's composition is just as meaningful as our own. Let us embrace the differences and learn to tolerate the diversity. Being different does not make us better or worse, just different. And it's ok to be different.

So whether it's teachers in the classroom or parents in the home, we have a common responsibility to cultivate the feeling of acceptance in our young people. Tolerating each other's diversity will make us stronger. Loving each other will make us eternal.

Statement – Adam

The late Reverend Ralph W. Sockman once said, "The test of courage comes when we are in the minority. The test of tolerance comes when we are in the majority."

Some of us have come here to Sea Cliff's Memorial Park because we are tolerant. Some of us have come here because we are courageous. Some of us have come here because we are both.

It is clear, however, that all of us who have come here believe in one thing: the complete and utter acceptance of people of all nationalities, ethnicities, races, genders and sexual orientation.

We do not fear difference, but celebrate it. We do not silence diversity, but offer it a chance to speak. We do not demand uniformity from variance, but encourage divergent thinkers and independent minds.

We welcome all individuals and are proud to do so. Here at Memorial Park, the citizens of Sea Cliff and the community at large should remember what we stand for: peace, justice, acceptance and equality for all.

Songs

1. Imagine – John Lennon

2. Let It Be -- The Beatles

3. We The People – Adam
There are some days in this life
when we see hate, destruction and strife.
And it helps us question who we want to be.
And sometimes, when we're lost, we can let the victims pay the cost
For trying to be exactly who they're supposed to be.
Well ain't it time for a little peace and harmony

We the people, must all stand together.
We the people, must demand something better.
We the people, must seek peace and find toleration or
We the people, won't survive as a nation.

I wouldn't know just how he feels,
Unless I felt the soles of his heels
As I walked forth as a true minority.
Well it seems our rights are done if we let majority rule run
Without some acceptance, who are we going to be?
That may be o.k. with you, but it's not where I want to be.

We the people, must all stand together.
We the people, must demand something better.
We the people, must seek peace and find toleration or
We the people, won't survive as a nation.

Aftermath
Responses to the Sea Cliff Tolerance Rally

Date: Sat, 29 Sep 2007, 22:12
Subject: (no subject)

225 To Karin from Constance & Gabe

Dear Karin and Doug,
Thank you so much for what your work and care brought to us all today in Sea Cliff. What you helped bring together and create has shed light and peace in many lives and in countless ones to come because of those affected today. We appreciate your caring and leadership and congratulate you on communicating your guidelines so that what needed to be focused on was rightly kept in the center.
We are off to C'town tomorrow until next Monday. It will be good to tell the girls all about it and our daughter was glad she was with us today also.
Love from Constance & Gabe

Date: Sun, 30 Sep 2007, 06:00
Subject: last thoughts

226 To Karin from The Rev. Dr. G. Shane Hibbs

Hello Karin,
I want to thank you for the opportunity to speak to your crowd yesterday. Sea Cliff is very fortunate to have strong leaders like yourself. Please let me know if there is ANYTHING that I can do for you and your community.
Grace and Peace,
The The Rev. Dr. G. Shane Hibbs

Date: Sun, 30 Sep 2007 09:10:58 -0400
Subject: rally

227 To Karin From: Mandy

Hi Karin
Just a word of thanks to you for putting this all together, even with such mean spirited opposition. Here was an opportunity to show solidarity instead of divisiveness and you did a great job.
Thanks
Mandy

Date: Sun, 30 Sep 2007, 13:30
Subject: Re: Niemoeller
228 To Karin from the Smiths

We thought the rally went great!!!!.. thanks for having the thought and courage to put this together... We were honored to be there with everyone

Date: Sun, 30 Sep 2007, 13:22
Subject: The Work Continues...LOVE has never been a popular movement in these yet to be
United States.
(James Baldwin said that!)

229 To Karin from Luke

Yup, as you all know, it's our 25th anniversary. What a great year it's been. Two guys in love for twenty five years! Some say it's like dog years when your LGBT. You're a survivor. Not all get that chance! Some of you may not recall that we both endured a hate crime attack in Bayshore, Long Island in the late 80's. We were spit upon, windows of the van punched by young Irish Catholic lads in their early twenties who threatening to kill us. **We got off lightly.**

Ahh yes. So that's what love can visit upon you in America! We remember the rally for Dix Hills, Long Island Resident Steen Keith Fenrich (1981-2000). Once again Long Islanders gathered and walked Huntington's Main Street, a heartbeat drum sounding in my hands, in honor of the memory of young Steen's life, potential, and his murder at the hands of his Dad related to his father's homophobia.

And then last month, in a beautiful hamlet overlooking Long Island Sound two of our sisters get attacked in September.

So when the real estate woman who keeps some of our Long Island crew connected sent her email that there was to be a rally, I chose to return to America's high street to add my body to the fray. In my Amnesty International tee shirt with the Pink Triangle that's now an LGBT symbol of pride I stood remembering how that triangle was put on LGBT folk who were incinerated or worked to death in the Holocaust for whom they loved. On the back of the shirt it says: **"LOVE IS A BASIC HUMAN RIGHT"**.

Perhaps if we all lived that, got rid of religious hatred globally that vilifies human love, well we'd strike at the root of where hatred often foments. I also wore a Marine hat in honor of my friend who wears the uniform of the United States and who is back for his second tour of Iraq-lands. I also wore the hat in honor of those LGBT WWII, Korean Era and Vietnam and other era LGBT veteran's I've had the honor of knowing who wore the uniform. We and they as taxpayers pay to keep terror from our own homeland, yet **terror is already here for minorities**. Someday, no matter who one loves, we as a Nation will put aside our phobias and change our laws to reflect that if our sons and daughters are willing to take a bullet or hopefully dodge road side bombs in the name of "freedom", we can simply chose to show we are a grateful nation and say allejuiah when those in uniform find love amidst the dangers of their military service for these yet to be United States.

At the rally, they sang IMAGINE. I thought of John in the etherworlds smiling down upon us above Long Island Sound. And Yoko, who over the years has been an advocate of the divine feminine. I shall never forget how she witnessed my walk with the man I love. Too, her song **Everyman/Everywoman** that celebrates human love. And having the rally close with her husband's former band's tune **Let It Be**. Can America let LGBT people be?! Let's make it happen!

And there was the woman and her husband from Sea Cliff who've loved their village, well, their home there of 40 years. And how that woman envisioned calling into being todays vigil. For such courage and community organizing she endured hate mail for that vision to gather human community and dispell the notion that her hometown was a place of intolerance. **Bless her courage** and that of the man who walks life with her. They both shared their admonition that Sea Cliff is a place of inclusion, not exclusion.

And those around the Nation and in Sea Cliff who said that maybe it was drunkeness on the part of the two women who were attacked. **You know they WERE in a bar! Reminds me of the old: "Well you know, they deserved violence because they dressed provocatively!" around women being at risk for rape.**

Thanks for the Dad who teaches seventh graders who wrote a song about constitutional freedoms and if we forget the notion of **WE THE PEOPLE** we may just lose our Nation.

And the Unitiarian Minister in the rainbow sash who strives to keep his Long Island Congregation as welcoming as I remember it's always been. And a Methodist Church of Sea Cliff church member talking about Christianity and her faith being welcoming, and another minister talking about the fact that we have to see that there is one way...**respect for humanity**.

And the fellow who in grad school said that LGBT kids needed a home, a safe space on Long Island so he dreamt it and he built that home with the help of others and soon he will look to honor Long Island's LGBT elders which is so needed! He admonished us not to forget that marriage rights remain important to all humans; as well as the fact that we really need to make sure our transgender brothers and sisters are not stripped from ENDA legislation **in the next few days** because of Americas ongoing puritannical shame dancing in the Capitol.

And the lad who played the guitar and live and on the spot figured out the chords of **Let It Be**. I thanked him for his musicianship and shared with him about the fact that teen kids can find direction and solace through that organization **PFLAG** or **Parents and Friends of Lesbians and Gays** which provides foundational education to parents of gay folk and gay folk themselves that **FACT: HUMANS ARE LOVED AND LOVEABLE AND DON'T LET ANYONE TELL YA DIFFERENT.**

So here we were AGAIN, on the village green, on the High Street...**where the work continues**. Thank you all ye brave souls of Sea Cliff and Long Island for sounding your chants of inclusion under the open sky! At the next rally maybe we'll sing with passion Mr. Bernstein's song, (what a great gay composer he was), from his West Side Story: ..."I **wanna LIVE in America!"**

If you'd like to say thank you to the sister who organized the vigil, she is the person above to whom this email is addressed. You can hit reply to all or just send her a personal note, share your views as an lgbt person or as a straight ally. Some Additional Resources:

Sea Cliff Bias Attack Of Former "Top Chef" Contestant
http://www.villagevoice.com/blogs/runninscared/archives/2007/09/fo rmer_top_chef.php

Arrest In Bias Attack In Sea Cliff
http://www.villagevoice.com/blogs/runninscared/archives/2007/09/li_ cops_make_bu.php

http://www.stophate.us/memorials/steen.html

Date: Sun, 30 Sep 2007, 21:59
Subject: tolerance in Park

230 To Karin from Sophia

Karin...I thought you were OUTSTANDING Saturday! What a lovely eloquent speech you made. You got right into everyone's heart ...I figure there must have been about 200 people there at least...I hope your words are repeated in the papers for all to hear or rather, see. Congratulations on a job very well done.

Doug's comments were also very good and very sweet...You make perfect sweethearts.

I'm sorry that Leo and I had to leave early...we had guests from out of town (connecticut) and I had to pull dinner together so they could get going...

Again, you were terrific!..........Sophia

Date: Mon, 1 Oct 2007, 09:24
Subject: Your statement

231 To Karin from Sarah, Human Rights Campaign

Karin, I, unfortunately, was pulled out of town for work at the end of the week, and I needed to be in NYC during the day Saturday. I got back to Sea Cliff by 5:45 on Saturday. Why did I think Memorial Park was the one near Tupelo Honey??

I apologize for not being in attendance, although I did distribute your fliers at our Wed cocktail event.

How did it go? Did [County Legislator] show up? I see she was listed to speak.

Sarah

Date: Mon, 01 Oct 2007, 09:40
Subject: rally

232 To Karin from Brenda

Hey Karin, just wanted to thank you for putting together the rally on Saturday. It was a very beautiful event, and I was so thrilled to be there. Wonderful energy, such powerful speeches...it was inspiring, and so are you!

I'm sorry the media didn't see it as worthy of coverage...I guess they wanted more controversy! The *News12* people actually said to me on the phone, "Will there be a counter demonstration?" I'm afraid that's what they were looking for.

So, regardless, it was lovely and touching and I'm so glad to have been there and to have met you!

Warm wishes,

Brenda

Date: Mon, 01 Oct 2007, 12:02
Subject: Rally program & purpose

233 To Karin from Rev. Owen

Thanks again for organizing this event. I was glad to have the opportunity to participate. Rev. Owen

234 To Karin from Miles

W.J. Bryant would be proud. Fine speeches, and nicely meshed in a
way that kept from stepping on each other's lines.
Miles

235 To Adam from Karin

Adam, I'm about to send a letter to the editors of the local papers. Do
you want to sign it, as well?
Karin

To the editor
More than 100 of us gathered for a community rally on Sept. 29 in Sea
Cliff to affirm our embrace of diversity and commitment to tolerance.
This was a necessary and powerful statement that has relevance far
beyond specific local events, perceptions and attitudes.
These are dangerous times for minorities and for the gay community, in
particular, because for many years now, the Republican Party, the
Christian Right and the conservative media have made demonizing the
most vulnerable populations among us—the gay and immigrant
communities—official public policy. Like it or not, this has set the tone
and context for widespread intolerance—the assault in Sea Cliff being
merely one of an increasing number of bias crimes all over the country.
Opposing gay rights and immigrant rights has become a sure-fire means
of scaring Americans into supporting and electing candidates. This scape
goating and fear-mongering is cleverly concealed behind pious slogans
like "family values," "moral majority," and "sanctity of marriage." Mitt
Romney recently called it: "defending the family." None of our elected
officials or candidates, Republicans or Democrats, dare challenge the
illogic and thinly veiled bigotry of these code words. It is up to all of us
who love what is best about this country, its promise of equality and
tolerance, to speak up individually and collectively.
One hundred individuals spoke up and made a resoundingly positive
statement in Sea Cliff's Memorial Park on Sept. 29. One Sea Cliff
resident made a statement with his campaign to discourage residents
from attending what he called a "pro-gay rally." Sea Cliff residents made
a statement by not attending. One resident, impersonating a village

official (without being able to spell his name right), made a statement by sending us hate mail.
We think our rally in support of diversity, tolerance and community was by far the most positive and inspiring statement.

(As expected, both Adam and Doug discourage me from sending the above letter. No matter. It felt great to write it. I subsequently write an un-political letter, below.)

Date: Mon, 1 Oct 2007, 17:46
Subject: To the editor (SENT)

236 To *The Glen Cove Record Pilot* & *The Gold Coast Gazette* from Karin

To the editor,
More than 100 of us gathered for a community rally on Sept. 29 in Sea Cliff's beautiful Memorial Park to affirm our embrace of diversity and commitment to tolerance. This was a necessary and powerful statement that has relevance far beyond specific local events, perceptions and attitudes. My thanks to all who joined us and special thanks to the participants who expressed themselves so eloquently, in music and words, about diversity and community, equality and tolerance. Thanks to Adam, fellow organizer, speaker and singer/songwriter extraordinaire, whose original composition, "We, the People," moved many of us to tears; to singer, Lorraine, and guitarist, Will, for their stirring renditions of John Lennon's "Imagine" and the Beatles' "Let It Be." Thanks to speakers Doug, Rev. Owen of the Unitarian Universalist Fellowship: the Sea Cliff Methodist Church: Mary of the National Organization for Women: David Kilmnick of the L.I. Gay and Lesbian Youth: Dr. Hibbs of the Long Island Community Fellowship, and to our Nassau County Legislator, who spoke simply as a mother about the need for teaching and modeling tolerant behavior. All of us, more than one hundred strong, who love our country and its promise of equality for all, made a resoundingly positive statement on Sept. 29 in support of diversity, tolerance and community.
Karin Barnaby

Date: Mon, 1 Oct 2007, 18:46
Subject: Debriefing

237 To Angela from Karin, follow up to telephone call

Hi Angela,
Sorry I couldn't talk. I'm off to chorus in a little while, but I thought I'd

send a copy of the program & the statements of the three SC participants. I can send you Dr. Hibbs' and Rev. Owen's statements, if you like. [County Legislator] was there from start to finish and spoke so simply & wonderfully as a mother, not at all as a politician. Also, I'm including my letter to the editors of the local papers. Finally, I'm including the letter I would have liked to send, but which I will save for some opportune moment at some later date--which remains btw. you and me for now.

You were a wonderful support and coach from far away PR. Thank you for all your help. It was a godsend. I'll call tomorrow.

Karin

Date: Mon, 1 Oct 2007, 18:55
Subject: SC rally

238 To 50 contacts from Karin

"More than 100 of us gathered for a community rally on Sept. 29 in Sea Cliff's beautiful Memorial Park to affirm our embrace of diversity and commitment to tolerance. This was a necessary and powerful statement that has relevance far beyond specific local events, perceptions and attitudes. . . "

Date: Mon, 1 Oct 2007, 22:10:20 -0400
Subject: Sea Cliff Rally

239 To Karin from Drew

Dear Karin,

Congratulations... Was unable to attend but, drove by on the way back to help at work, noticed the police and was concerned...

Drew

Date: Mon, 1 Oct 2007, 22:49
Subject: RE: Debriefing

240 To Karin from Angela

Karin,

Your email and the associated attachments were the last email messages I read before this reply (and then I'm trotting off to bed).

People came to the rally for different reasons - whether they were impacted by the incident because they're Sea Cliff residents, or sexual minorities or both or neither (I'm thinking of my dear friend Mary who spoke on behalf of NOW). I wanted to thank you for creating a space for solidarity and healing regardless of what the connection was.

Even though I wasn't at the rally, knowing that it occurred has brought me a peace that has been missing since the incident. I speak for almost every sexual minority woman I know when I say we don't like to ask for help. We value our privacy and we focus on our abilities, not our liabilities or disabilities. I want you and the other rally organizers to know that the solidarity afforded by the rally was appreciated in ways that only other people who have experienced oppression will understand. Oppression may sound like an extreme choice of language, but it can be as insidious as devaluing work because it's done by a woman, or being denied something you would be entitled to if you were a man/a citizen/a heterosexual/a Caucasian/ and so on, or it can be as irrational as our federal government having two sets of books for married couples - one for married not taxable, and one for married taxable. It's obvious to me from our conversations that I am preaching to the choir, I know you get it! I just wanted you to know I appreciated all your efforts.

Looking forward to hearing your impressions and if there remains any way that I can be of further service.

Warmly,
Angela

Date: Tue, 2 Oct 2007, 11:49
Subject: Debriefing

241 To Angela from Karin

Angela,
I tried to call you but can't get through--not in service, etc., etc. When you get a chance, could you call me, please. Meanwhile, there is something I would ask, if it you feel comfortable doing it. Would you be willing to write a letter to the editors of our local papers re. your feelings/thoughts about the assault and rally, exactly as you expressed them in your very first and your most recent emails? The far-reaching reverberations of the assault within the lesbian and gay community and the significance of the rally—both emotional and symbolic—is a desperately needed perspective. It would be a powerful statement that would foster a deeper understanding.

Let me know,
Karin

Date: Tue, 2 Oct 2007, 12:50
Subject: letter to the editor

242 To Angela from Karin, follow up to phone conversation

Hi Angela,
If this is helpful, good; if not, just delete it.

You sounded so busy that I decided to try and help. Here's my suggestion for a letter to the editor, compiled of excerpts from your emails. Naturally, I deleted and added, where appropriate, to create a natural flow. If you should get your letter written the way you want it in time for this week's news cycle, send it asap (before this evening) to the *Glen Cove Record Pilot* and to the *Gold Coast Gazette*. Do not send it as an attachment but scroll the letter into the email text.

Thanks,
Karin

My suggestion:

"To the editor
Even though I wasn't at the rally, knowing that it occurred has brought me a peace that has been missing since the bias incident. I speak for almost every sexual minority woman I know when I say we don't like to ask for help. We value our privacy and we focus on our abilities, not our liabilities or disabilities. The solidarity afforded by the rally was appreciated in ways that only other people who have experienced oppression will understand. Oppression may sound like an extreme choice of language, but it can be as insidious as devaluing work because it's done by a woman, or being denied something you would be entitled to if you were a man/a citizen/a heterosexual/a Caucasian/and so on, or it can be as irrational as our federal government having two sets of books for married couples - one for married not taxable, and one for married taxable.
By organizing this community action, the village residents' response to this bias incident sends an incredibly powerful message that Sea Cliff is one, unified and diverse, multicultural community and that bias on its streets or against any of its citizens is not okay."

Date: Tue, 2 Oct 2007, 12:56
Subject: Press

243 To Karin from Angela

Karin,
I don't have access to the emails you're suggesting I work from here on my blackberry. Would it be possible for you to forward them to me, and I'll do it now, at the office?
Thanks!
Angela

244 To Angela from Karin

Your past emails:

Your first email: Sun, 23 Sep 2007 12:29:14 -0400:
"Hi Karin,
As per my conversation with Sarah, I'd like to introduce myself and offer
to be of service in preparing for the upcoming rally. . ."

Today's email: Mon, 1 Oct 2007, 22:49 :
"Karin,
Your email and the associated attachments were the last email messages
I read before this reply . . ."

245 To Karin from *GC Record Pilot* editor
hi, karin...
is this just for my information or do you want it printed?
thanks,
Editor, *GC Record Pilot*

246 To Editor, *GC Record Pilot* from Karin
I thought I'd sent it as a letter to the editor. That's how I intended it.
Definitely want it printed.
Thanks,
Karin

247 To Karin from Editor, *GC Record Pilot*
okey dokey...

248 To Adam from Karin
Hi Adam,
Thought you'd like to see this letter to the editor from Angela.
So good.
Karin

249 To Karin from Angela

Karin,

Thank you for suggesting a letter to the editor, and especially for this draft. Will you let me know if it's published in either paper? Warmly,

Angela

Angela's letter, as it appeared in the local newspapers:

There in Spirit

As a former Glen Head resident, I tried to attend the rally in Sea Cliff on Sept. 29. Although I couldn't get there, just knowing it occurred has given me a peace that had been missing since national media coverage sent shock waves beyond the Village borders. In times like these, silence is not neutral.

Speaking on behalf of almost every sexual minority woman I know, we don't like to ask for help; we value our privacy and we focus on our abilities, not our liabilities or disabilities. This community action was appreciated in ways that only others who have experienced oppression will understand. Oppression may sound like an extreme choice of language, but it can be as insidious as devaluing work because it's done by a woman, or being denied something you would be otherwise entitled to if you were a citizen, a heterosexual, a Caucasian, and so on; or it can be as irrational as our federal government having two sets of books for married couples - one for married not taxable, and one for married taxable.

I would like to acknowledge the Village of Sea Cliff for permitting this rally and its organizers for breaking the silence. It sent a powerful, visible message of solidarity that Sea Cliff is a unified and diverse multicultural community and that bias on its streets or against any of its citizens is not okay.

250 To Adam from Karin

Hi Adam,
I'm forwarding all the emails I've gotten. Also, Gail approached me at the rally before we started and whispered in my ear that she was wrong and we were right. She called today & we had a long conversation about what a fine effort and success the rally was. She requested and I sent her our--your, Doug's & my-- statements.
I told Doug at dinner tonight that I had a sense of *High Noon* about our whole effort, including the strong desire to throw the sheriff's badge on the table, as a final symbolic image & gesture of my disappointment and disgust. Like you wanting to resign from everything, I don't want to do a darn thing for the village right now either. There must be a strong archetypal dynamic to what we did. But I'm feeling better & better about what we did :-)
Karin

251 To Karin from Adam

My God, I don't check my email for a few hours and look what happens. I'm happy to say that I've been listening to the new Bruce Springsteen cd which just came out. The man has so much integrity it is ridiculous. Nice album.
Anyway, it was great to read all of the comments. You really did a wonderful job. The rally was well managed and eloquent. What more could you ask for? I'm still debating about whether to write a letter and whether to resign. I am supremely disappointed in the Village Board. I think the best way to go about it might be to attend a Village Board meeting and publicly call them out. I don't know if they had a meeting tonight or not, but maybe Monday might have to be the night.
Congratulations, again, on a job well done.
Peace and Pay it Forward,
Adam

252 To Adam from Karin

And congratulations to you on a job well done. You were such a source
of encouragement and strength. I would suggest you definitely write your
letter and put it in an envelope. It is deeply satisfying. I think that must
have been the purpose of my first, unsent letter to the editor that you and
Doug so wisely shot down. Eventually I will send that first letter. You'll
have to see whether you will send yours or not.

I'll have to check out Springsteen. That good, eh?

Someone told me yesterday that they overheard a conversation about the
rally where one young mother was telling another how terrific your song
was & that everyone had tears in their eyes. Yesss!

Karin

253 To John from Karin

I understand that you decided not to attend the rally based on the notice
that appeared in the *Record Pilot* on Sept. 27. For the record, I did not put
that in. I submitted a simple flier with the words "Diversity - Tolerance -
Community - Sea Cliff" on it. The *Gold Coast Gazette* published it as
received. I don't know why the *Record Pilot* chose to do what it did.

Karin

254 To Karin from Elaine

Karin,

You accomplished something admirable and excellent. I was sorry not to
be there, but we were already booked for that time. Thank you for what
you have done for our community.

Sincerely,

Elaine

255 To Zoe from Karin

Hi Zoe,

Hope you had a wonderful NYC visit with your children. Below is my
summary of the rally that I sent to the local papers. I'm attaching the
rally statements by Doug, Adam and me, as well as forwarding a letter

from a woman that says it all. I encouraged her to send it to the local papers which she did.

xo Karin Barnaby

Date: Wed, 3 Oct 2007, 11:27
Subject: Re: rally

256 To Karin from Zoe

I'm feeling proud of all who turned out and especially you, Karin, who got to learn one more time that no good deed goes unpunished. Of course I wish there had been three thousand people in Memorial Park, but the ones who were there were the right people and I like to think that each one represented the feelings of many more. Thank you, thank you! Zoe

Date: Wed, 3 Oct 2007, 09:50
Subject: SC rally

257 To Karin from Rachel
You did it Karen!!!
love Rachel

Date: Wed, 03 Oct 2007, 21:12
Subject: reactions

258 To Karin from Adam
I'm pretty much decided that I'm going to resign from the [. . .] committee and the [. . .] committee. I will write a specific email to [trustee] explaining why and I will send a more generic one to the members of the committees explaining why I quit.

That is great to hear about the song. Today I sang for about 3 hours in school. I wrote several songs for our exploration unit and sang them to all of my classes. It was a lot of fun.

As far as Springsteen goes, he is not for everyone, but I would basically give my life for the guy. I would start with Born To Run, move on to Darkness on the Edge of Town, dabble in Born in the USA and get lost in The Rising (the first artistic response to 9/11-You're Missing is especially moving). Anyway, his lyrics are incredible, his band is phenomenal and his live shows are legendary. I think I am actually going to scalp tickets to his upcoming show at MSG and go by myself. That is how much I love his music.

I hope you are well,
Adam

Reprimand #3

In this email to Doug and Village administrators, Natalie reminds everyone that I had stolen the group's contact list and had promised never to use it again. She scolds all of us for sending our dirty laundry—the hate mail and disclaimers—to group members all over Long Island, and warns us to stop our fraudulent use of the list. She intends to investigate the legal ramifications of our offense.
Doug emails an answer, since this email was sent to him, but not me.

Date: Tue, 2 Oct 2007, 21:32
Subject: Emails dated 27 Sep.

259 To Natalie from Doug

I do not know what is behind your persistence to pursue your attacks and accusations against my wife, Karin, but in the future if you have something to say to me, call me on the telephone and I will gladly tell you what I think of your statements.
Douglas

Reprimand #4

In Natalie's opinion, the shameful emails—the hate mail and our disclaimers—have besmudged the group's reputation and violated members' privacy. They've done more damage to Sea Cliff's image than the news coverage of the bias attack. I have done irreparable harm, and destroyed eight years of the group's work.
I email an answer.

Date: Sat, 20 Oct 2007 15:26
Subject: honesty

260 To Natalie from Karin

Natalie
I wonder if, by now, you've mustered the honesty and courage to realize how wrong you were in making any number of assumptions about me, my motivations and actions in connection with the Sea Cliff rally. Here are some of your publicly emailed, misinformed, false and/or just plain nasty accusations:

- the contact list was stolen by Karin Barnaby
- an unknown member of our board gave Karin Barnaby, without

the [organization's] permission, our user name and password to access our contact lists containing your email address . . . this heinous breech [correct spelling: breach] of privacy and misuse of the [organization's] records.

- abuse of the [organization's] records
- fraudulent use of the contact list.
- the [organization's] reputation is being besmudged by the continued use of our contact list.
- the damage Karin caused the [organization] may be irreparable.
- Karin Barnaby has used the rally as a platform to bash one particular business.
- slanderous statements and actions against [bar]
- cast aspersions against a person or a business without unequivocal proof is in and of itself criminal.

First, every time you send an [organization] email you are putting all the members' names and email addresses in the public domain. No one needs permission, a user name or password to access the list; no one has to steal it or commit fraud. At worst, people who receive unwanted emails as a result of use by "third parties" simply delete them. It is my understanding that you yourself have used the [organization's] email list for non-organization purposes in the past. For what it's worth, there is a way of sending group emails that obscures or blinds the other recipients' names & addresses. You might want to look into it if you want to stop yourself from inadvertently committing a "heinous breech of privacy" each time you send emails in the future,

Second, I have never bashed, slandered, cast aspersions or acted in any criminal way against [bar] a person or business. It couldn't be further from my mind to do so. As soon as I became aware that a rally at or near [bar] might be perceived as a criticism of the bar, rather than of the bias assault, I relocated the rally to Memorial Park. I never mentioned [bar] in any press release. I sent out clear participants guidelines and screened all rally speakers' statements to make sure [bar] was not mentioned.

Finally, it is one thing for you to want to think ill of me on the basis of your past misperceptions and false assumptions. It is quite another for you to publicly denounce and smear me on the basis of your present misperceptions and false assumptions.
Don't do it again. I will not tolerate such behavior in the future.
Karin

Reprimand #5

I am guilty of: *an absolute lack of honesty . . . cpmplete(?) cowardice . . .
unscrupulous and unethical deeds . . . piracy . . . thievery . . . unethical and
immoral acts and cunning . . . deceitful actions. . . publicly bashing a bar.*

I have: *a devious and scurritous(?), perverted and demented mind.*

I am: *unethical, immoral, devious, narcisstic(?) . . . devoid of feelings of
remorse or guilt . . . anti-social.*

Date: Sat, 6 Oct 2007, 12:03
Subject: Thanks

261 To the *Gold Coast Gazette* from Karin

My heatfelt thanks for covering the rally--and for giving it the second
page. I know there was much going on last weekend and it probably
wasn't easy to juggle events, but you sent Steve (reporter) to cover the
whole thing. Thank you for that. Also, thank you for printing the letter
from Angela. I encouraged her to send it to you and the *Record-Pilot*
because it expressed the perspective and reaction of the lesbian & gay
community to the bias assault. God, it is so tough to be a minority of
any kind!
How much of the event did Steve actually record & would it be possible
to copy/transfer the audio and photos onto CDs? It would mean so
much since I totally forgot to think of recording/filming the rally. I
would gladly pay whatever is involved.
I'm compiling all the emails into a kind of chronicle of how this initiative
began and evolved into such a moving and inspiring community
statement--a kind of "Civil Action 101." With the exception of a few
phone calls and the valuable press coverage, the rally was entirely
organized via emails--everything from the first mention of the assault, to
arguments for and against, to hate mail, to individuals one-by-one
coming aboard, to final thank-yous. I purposely did not invite public
officials, activist groups, etc. because I felt it was absolutely essential that
everyone search their own hearts and consciences re. supporting,
ignoring, rationalizing or opposing the rally. It was quite a litmus test of
attitudes, with some pleasant, as well as disappointing surprises. We'll see
what comes of it.
Thanks again for supporting this from beginning to end.
Karin

News update: two arrests

Date: Tue, 13 Nov 2007 13:44
Subject: Follow up to Sea Cliff Incident...

262 To 10 recipients from Angela, CC: 7 recipients

Just a quickie update....

The investigation into the Sea Cliff crime remains open and active. This is being investigated as a hate crime and will be prosecuted as such. There is a game plan and there should be further developments within the next 2-3 weeks. The Commissioner reiterated his commitment to fully pursue this case and all other bias incidents in the County. He has made public statements that specifically included our (LGBT) communities. A task force has also been created.

At this point, I'm comfortable with the ways things are moving along. I hope you will pass along this info to those who inquire, so that opinions can be based on fact. If community members think there are other things that should be happening, but are not, I will be happy to pass the feedback along.

I'll update you when I know more which I expect will be in a few weeks.

Thanks,

Angela

Two Charged in Suspected Anti-Gay Attack Involving 'Top Chef' Contestant Who Pressed for Arrests
The Associated Press

Sea Cliff, NY, November 18, 2007

Two women have been charged in the case of a former contestant on Bravo's "Top Chef" who said she was beaten by attackers yelling anti-gay slurs over Labor Day weekend. Nassau County police announced the arrests on Saturday after Josie Smith-Malave, who was featured on the second season of the reality show, had accused investigators last week of not pursuing her case vigorously.

Smith-Malave, who is openly lesbian, said she and three other women were assaulted by about a dozen people after being told to leave a Sea Cliff bar on Sept. 1, according to police. The attackers yelled slurs about the women's perceived sexual orientation, spat on them and hit them, police said.

Melissa Trimarchi, 21, was charged with misdemeanor assault, police said. She was released on an appearance ticket until a Nov. 30 court date. No working telephone number could be found for Trimarchi at the Sea Cliff address police gave, and they didn't know whether she had an attorney. Elizabeth Borroughs, 20, was charged with aggravated harassment, also a misdemeanor. She also was released on an appearance ticket and is due in court on Friday. A woman who identified herself as Borroughs at the Glen Cove address police gave said Saturday that she didn't know about the case. Police were unsure whether she had a lawyer.

A homeless man, Matthew W. Walli, 20, was accused of stealing a victim's video camera during the attack. He was arrested in September on a charge of robbery as a bias crime. His lawyer's name and the status of his court case were not immediately available on Sunday.

Smith-Malave's lawyer, Yetta Kurland, rapped the investigation Friday, saying police hadn't gone after all suspects vigorously and had failed "to treat the vicious attack ... as the violent hate crime that it was."

Kurland didn't immediately respond to a telephone message left at her office late Saturday. Smith-Malave, a 32-year-old Miami native, is a former sous-chef for the Marlow and Sons restaurant in Brooklyn. She has played for the New York Sharks of the Independent Women's Football League.

Lessons learned

1. There are many decent, good-hearted people in Sea Cliff.
2. There are a few nasty people in Sea Cliff.
3. While friends and neighbors may not think and feel as I do, some complete strangers do.
4. Every encouraging word counts.
5. People's preconceptions and prejudices render them impervious to facts and logic.
6. A community will rally around its own, regardless of their guilt or innocence.
7. "Outsiders" who disrupt a community's status quo are suspect, regardless of their guilt or innocence.
8. When members of a minority are victimized, silence on the part of the majority is not neutral.

Last thoughts

In Billings, Montana (pop. 90,000), when someone threw a rock at a menorah in a Jewish family's window, about 10,000 businesses and residences displayed menorahs in their windows, in a show of solidarity with the victims. In Sea Cliff, New York (pop. 5,000), when lesbian women were assaulted by a group of young people, about 100-150 people attended a tolerance rally in a show of solidarity with the victims.

Last words

Some weeks after the Sea Cliff Tolerance Rally, when I went to delete the emails accumulated, I was struck by their candor, thoughtfulness and drama. The emails represented a dynamic cross-section of our Village, as well as of the extended online community that had coalesced around this issue. I decided to save them. Organized into a coherent whole, the email chronicle offered a compelling documentation of the aftermath of the alleged bias attack in our Village. I sent the chronicle to those individuals who had encouraged and supported the rally. Their responses inspired me to try to publish it. Having received dozens of rejections from agents and having received and rejected overtures from a dubious online publisher, I opted to sellf-publish.

Date: Sat, March 14, 2009 1:26:57 PM
Subject: SC Rally chronicle

263 From Karin to Adam

Hi Adam,

I've finally gotten my email chronicle of the Sea Cliff rally publication-ready. I was wondering if you would like to see the finished product? I think it is quite compelling. The volume is about 100 pages. Because it is an email chronicle and formatting is so important, I would have to send it as an attachment and I know that is a problem for some. For now, I'll scroll in the preface, below. Let me know if you'd like to see the entire volume.

If I haven't made it clear enough, you were the most important presence, support, co-conspirator throughout. I don't know how the rally would ever have become such a fine effort without you.

Best wishes,
Karin

Date: Saturday, March 14, 2009, 4:05 PM
Subject: Re: SC Rally chronicle

264 From Adam to Karin

Karin, I am SO happy for you. I can't wait to read it.

I'm really thankful that I know you, Karin. Remember, I may have helped, but you got the ball rolling and put it together. The first step is

always the most important and you should be so proud of yourself in knowing that you were the one with the most courage.
Can't wait.
Adam

265 From Karin to Adam

Aw shucks. As you once said to me: you're the goods, Adam. Here's the chronicle. I imagine you have a pretty savvy computer that can handle large files, but if you need me to break up the text, let me know.
Karin

266 From Adam to Karin

I couldn't put it down, or, close the computer. Definitely didn't remember all that had transpired. It was an amazing page turner. I was involved and still wanted to know how it would turn out. Would love to talk to you about this. Reading it over made me remember how good it felt to do the right thing. I really think you have the makings of something special. I could see my students buying it at the Glen Cove Holocaust and Tolerance Museum.
Must sleep.
Adam

267 From Angela to Karin

Hi Karin,
I just completed reading through your chronicle. I laughed, I cried - I was surprised that your experience could be so resonant to me, but it was most interesting how reading your chronicle normalized an aspect of my own experience that I hadn't ever considered before. Specifically, it was never really clear to me before how individuals could and would go to extreme lengths to attack the messenger to deride and derail the message!! How very enlightening. I wouldn't have gotten it without actually being walked through your own experience step by step. For this reason alone, I can think of a dozen people off the top of my head, who could personally benefit from reading this! Please let me know when and

how you make this available to the general public so that I can pass it along as recommended reading :)
Warmly,
Angela

" We need to be open to the possibility that human knowledge—what we know, what we value, what we consider important—may change when former outsiders become full partners in knowledge production." Londa Schiebinger

Date: Wed, February 17, 2010 7:20:49 PM
Subject: different attachment application

268 From Brenda to Karin

Well, Karin, I just read the whole thing. What a brave, strong woman you are. This N. person is so disturbing. I dare say that she is a homophobe and this WHOLE thing with you is a cover for her bigotry. I can't know it, but I'd bet on it.
The reverend Owen is my reverend at the UUFH. I'm so proud to call him the leader of my religious community.
I wish so much that there was more press coverage. It merited it, that's for sure.
I am proud to have been there, and to have met you. You remind me of what is best in people, and what I love about Sea Cliff!
Best,
Brenda

Zoe had the first word in this chronicle. Hers is also the last word here.

Date: Sun, February 21, 2010 2:29:21 PM
Subject: Chronicle of the SC tolerance rally

269 From Zoe to Karin

Hi Karin,
I read this straight through and found it riveting. More thoughts flew through my head than I can put on paper when packing for a trip. Did I overdramatize in the beginning, influencing you to feel dramatic action was called for? Why did I believe every word I read in the newspaper, when I know better? Perhaps the appropriate headline for what happened at Partners' is A Bunch of People Behaving Badly, and that includes Gay-bashing. You were committed to doing the right thing, even when it became less clear what the right thing was.
What to make of all the good people in Sea Cliff who didn't turn out?
For a lot of them, it was just not their issue. When our church committee

does a program on equal rights for GLBT folks, it's not a big draw. Others couldn't/didn't follow the fast-paced action.

I can see, in retrospect, how right-thinking people could feel that a protest outside Partners' before all the facts were in was not the right call. When you started promoting a rally in a park with a positive goal, could they have felt that was like, well, putting lipstick on a pig?

The impressive thing is what you pulled off. That was grass-roots organizing at its best, and hats off to you and the other people who worked hard under pressure and produced something very good. We miss you and Doug still, and I think you both represent what's good about Sea Cliff.

Love,

Zoe

CPSIA information can be obtained
at www.ICGtesting.com
Printed in the USA
BVOW09s1115110517

483771BV00001B/45/P